W9-DDN-649

ShortTrack CEO

How Mid-Market CEOs Apply Four Critical Concepts to Achieve Their Personal Goals

Contact the authors at **www.ShortTrackCEO.com** or 901-653-2930.

Praise for ShortTrack CEO

"ShortTrack CEO offers practical, powerful techniques which can transform your business if properly implemented."

—Michael L. Ducker
Chief Operating Officer and President, International
FedEx Express

"The concepts articulated in ShortTrack CEO have been important and effective tools for the leaders of a dynamic private company in which we have made a significant equity investment."

—R. Brad Martin
Chairman, RBM Venture Company
Retired Chairman & CEO, Saks Incorporated

Preface

Despite having a common title, CEOs of mid-market companies—which we define as companies between $1 million and $100 million in revenue—have vastly different challenges from their counterparts at the enterprise and Fortune 500 level.

Fortune 500 CEOs have almost unlimited resources at their disposal, are constantly in the public eye, and can relatively easily measure their performance—by their stock price. These jobs are extremely difficult to obtain and most CEOs have been groomed for the position for upwards of 10 years, and, while they're high-pressure jobs, even some poor performers get a $100 million payday. Fortune 500 CEOs are the celebrities of the business world.

Mid-market CEOs have fewer resources, are rarely in the public eye, and cannot so easily measure their performance. Their jobs aren't nearly as difficult to obtain, and many mid-market CEOs haven't been groomed for their position at all. They're still high-pressure jobs, but it's a different type of pressure. Mid-market CEOs are also often invisible in the business world outside their local markets.

On the job, the differences are further amplified. Fortune 500 and enterprise CEOs (which we define as CEOs running companies over $100 million in revenue) have highly-skilled and well-trained executives to rely upon, large budgets, and an array of MBAs and consultants to deliver the information they need whenever they need it. Mid-market CEOs have a far smaller stable of executives. While an $80 million company will have more key executives than an $8 million company, the average mid-market company CEO has a CFO or financial executive, a VP of Sales, one or two operational executives, and two or three key managers.

The net result is that mid-market CEOs end up making far too many key business decisions based on instinct alone, instead of confirming or refuting their instinct with relevant information, as the CEOs at Fortune 500 companies do. While their instincts are typically good, there are far too many instances where gut instinct goes against the correct business decision. This causes mid-market companies to struggle executing the company strategy and the CEO's ultimate personal end goal.

The Forgotten Mid-Market Companies

The majority of the business materials published each year are focused on either general business concepts or specific stories and recommendations for the two other categories of businesses—enterprise corporations and small business owners/entrepreneurs.

The mid-market CEO is often ignored, unable to deploy the general concepts suggested by business thought-leaders, or to find significant value in the recommendations given to small business owners.

This book is written for that often-ignored mid-market CEO and is based on my and my co-authors' research and experiences as we've worked with 2,000 CEOs of mid-market companies over the last 10 years throughout the United States, Europe, and Australia.

Our experiences have yielded two highly intriguing discoveries:

1. Mid-market CEOs fall into five different categories, or "personas" as we'll call them, and the personal goals of each are distinctly different and directly affect how they can most effectively manage their company.

2. While mid-market CEOs have far fewer resources than do enterprise CEOs, there are four concepts we've discovered that, if embraced by mid-market CEOs, can enable them to overcome the majority of elements that cause their companies to struggle, and cause them to fall short of their personal goals. Furthermore, while implementing all four concepts should improve the value of any mid-market company, mid-market CEOs tend to have a specific attraction to the concepts based on their own persona—creating an individual formula for success.

We call the individual formulas for each CEO persona their ShortTrack — the pathway for the mid-market CEO to move directly from Point A (today) to Point B (their personal goal).

Our discoveries resulted from our many years of client work, which enabled us to access the hearts and minds of mid-market CEOs—fieldwork that cannot be replicated in the classroom or learned by analyzing data or statistics.

First I'll share the four concepts that you, a mid-market CEO, can embrace and bring to life to create a more valuable company:

1. Your CFO is not giving you all the numbers you need to confirm your everyday decisions.

2. You have the ability to take the guesswork out of managing your people.

3. You must win mind share to influence your market.

4. Your team must be able to clearly articulate your purpose and your vision.

Concept #1:

Your CFO is not giving you all the numbers you need to confirm your everyday decisions.

It's not difficult to quantify basic operational results from numbers on standard financial statements: profit and loss, assets, liabilities, and equity.

But what do these numbers really tell you?

Do these standard financial statements truly measure the value your operations are generating? Can you use them in real time to confirm or refute your or your teams' instincts, while making the constant operational decisions each month that impact your performance?

For example, if your team were to ask you any of the questions below, how long would it take to respond with a solid answer supported by firm dollar amounts?

- If we increase our prices 3%, will our revenue go up or down? What about our profits?

- What happens to our company value if we enter this new market?

- If we offer a 5% discount to our suppliers to pay net 10, does that improve the value of our company?

- Our input prices are rising. Should we lock in a fixed price? How can we quantify the impact on our business if we don't do this, and prices keep increasing?

- Can we afford this new equipment?

- Should we lower our prices to sell more and increase our revenue?

- How is this strategic investment affecting our financial performance?

- How are our staff costs tracking against revenue generation, and what impact will a 2% increase in productivity have on our cash flow and return?

To get the answers, do you refer to your P&L, your balance sheet, or your cash flow statement?

Of course you don't. Standard financial statements don't deliver answers to these questions.

But savvy mid-market CEOs learned long ago that there are plenty of numbers that can be extracted from these financial statements—hidden from plain view, but accessible—that can deliver the answers to these types of questions.

To get the numbers you and your team need to confirm everyday decisions, conduct the following activities (which we'll discuss in detail in the book):

1. Change your budgeting and forecasting methods from year-to-date or TTM, to 24 month rolling.

2. Manage your strategic investments in a J Curve register.

3. Build relevant financial modeling to get numerical answers to the questions you currently answer based on pure instinct.

Concept #2:
You have the ability to take the guesswork out of managing your people.

Have you ever hired a smart person with a strong resume and plenty of experience, expecting a certain level of performance, but ending up with something completely different? Do key members of your leadership team have certain traits that may be holding them back from achieving their full potential?

For most mid-market CEOs, the answer to both questions is a resounding *Yes*.

This is natural, as humans are imperfect creatures driven by emotion, beliefs, quirks, and irrationalities. The good news is that over the last 20 years scientific research has begun to unlock many of the complexities of human nature.

Today, mid-market CEOs have access to effective, scientifically proven employee assessment tools that enable them to sharpen management skills, strengthen team performance, identify hidden skills in employees, and remove the guesswork from the hiring process. These assessments are backed by decades of scientific research and have the capacity to:

- Identify and describe the facets of an employee's personality

- Identify leadership qualities and leadership style

- Determine an individual's natural reaction mode to environmental stimuli—their personal behavioral style

- Measure emotional intelligence—the ability to adjust to one's environment

Once thought of as a "soft skill," the ability to assess these characteristics is becoming more quantifiable in many professions—especially in leadership roles—and they play a significant role in overall job success.

To take the guesswork out of managing your people, conduct the following activities (which we'll discuss in detail in the book):

1. Map your people using a carefully chosen set of validated assessments.

2. Coach your people based on the findings.

3. Use a structured hiring system to get the right people on board and protect your people assets.

Concept #3:
You must win mind share to influence your market.

Years ago Peter Drucker, the father of business consulting, made a very profound observation:

◀◀ *Because the purpose of business is to create a customer, the business enterprise has two—and only two—basic functions: marketing and innovation. Marketing and innovation produce results; all the rest are costs. Marketing is the distinguishing, unique function of the business.*

Yet the marketing function is broad, challenging, and often misunderstood, especially at the mid-market level. Ask several people to define it and you'll probably get very different answers.

The Fortune 500 and savvy mid-market consumer products companies approach the marketing function from a fundamentally different angle from that of most mid-market companies:

They start with market research and devise a focused, comprehensive strategy to penetrate their market, build their brand, and win mind share before they enter a market.

The typical mid-market company is focused on sales, a tactical function of the marketing process, and gives little thought to researching the market, building a brand, and winning mind share. When you consider the mindset of the typical mid-market CEO, this makes sense; most were very skilled and well-trained engineers, salespeople, or finance people prior to starting their own company or taking over the top role.

To win mind share and influence your market, conduct the following activities (which we'll discuss in detail in the book):

1. Determine the mind share you want to win.

2. Create a brand strategy that embodies the mind share you seek to own.

3. Use a systematic approach for all your marketing and sales activities.

Concept #4:
Your team must be able to clearly articulate your purpose and your vision.

Your company's purpose is the single driver of all company activity. It's the reason you, the CEO, come to work each day; it's the reason the company exists—a reason that your leadership team can clearly articulate, and the market understands.

That's how it should be, but it's not true for many mid-market companies.

It's easy to think that the company purpose is to return profits to owners or shareholders; however, profits are simply the end result of well-run companies. An effective purpose reflects people's idealistic motivations for doing the company's work and doesn't just describe the organization's output or target customers; it captures the soul of the organization.

Great companies operate with a public purpose that is supported by a strong foundation. Company purpose and foundational work became very commonplace in Fortune 500 companies starting in the mid 1990s, much of it resulting from lengthy research and findings published by renown business authors, such as Jim Collins and Jerry Porras.

To clearly articulate your purpose and vision, conduct the following activities (which we'll discuss in detail in the book):

1. Clarify your purpose.

2. Define your core company values.

3. Build your supporting foundation infrastructure.

We discovered that many mid-market companies had already implemented bits and pieces of the concepts before we began working with them. This finding did not really surprise us, since the activities that support each concept are already part of the fabric of most Fortune 500 companies. While it's natural for good business practices of big companies to trickle down to mid-market companies, we learned that there's still a large gap between the two, leaving plenty of opportunity for mid-market CEOs to improve the way they run their companies.

The second major element of our discovery was that every mid-market CEO we encountered fell into one of five specific profiles, based on their personal goals. We call these the *CEO personas*:

1. **The Growth CEO** — You have a desire to move forward, to get bigger, to expand, to beat your competition and win the game. While this seems to be the logical profile of all CEOs, that isn't what we've experienced—approximately 30% of the CEOs we encounter are true 'growth CEOs.'

2. **The Hired Gun CEO** — You've been brought into a new company with the goal of making a short term, immediate impact. It's usually a turnaround or preparation for a company sale, and you have a big financial gain at stake and a reputation for being a turnaround expert. Approximately 15% of the CEOs we encounter fall into this persona.

3. **The Strategic CEO** — You're striving for a mid-term exit in 10 years. You're either a company founder, or you've run the company a long time—and you're focused on improving the business, to sell or transfer to a family member. Approximately 20% of the CEOs we encounter fall into this persona.

4.   **The Career CEO** — You're a new CEO taking on your first command and have achieved your dream role—you plan on being a CEO for multiple companies over your career. Approximately 10% of the CEOs we encounter fall into this persona.

5.   **The Auto-Pilot CEO** — You've achieved continued success with your business, but it still requires all your attention to operate the company at your desired level. You'd like to get the business to the point where it can perform at this level without your constant involvement, so you can work less and have more time for other activities. Approximately 25% of the CEOs we encounter fall into this persona.

And finally, we learned that each of the five CEO personas has the ability to embrace and implement the concepts in order to achieve their personal end goals. The CEOs didn't suggest the formulas to use—they became apparent throughout our work with them.

The ShortTrack for the Five Mid-Market CEO Personas

CEO Persona	Goal	ShortTrack
Growth CEO	Build a bigger company.	75% concept 3 + 15% concept 4 + 10% concept 1
Hired Gun CEO	Turn around a company in a short period of time.	65% concept 1 + 20% concept 3 + 15% concept 2
Strategic CEO	Build value for an exit within 6 to 10 years.	25% concept 1 + 25% concept 2 + 25% concept 3 + 25% concept 4
Career CEO	Enhance skills to be able to run other companies.	Focus on your weakest concepts.
Auto-Pilot CEO	Have existing company continue current performance with less time commitment.	Focus on your company's weakest concepts.

Our Background

My co-authors, Jim Sagar and Nick Setchell, and I have each devoted our careers to solving the challenges of mid-market companies—the "forgotten" companies of the business landscape.

Each of us was pursuing solutions independently in our areas of expertise for many years before we met: I as a former CEO training others in sales, leadership development, business foundational work, and people management; Jim in marketing and sales; and Nick in operational management.

Our paths crossed in 2006, and since then we've worked to organize and synchronize all our findings into a framework and solution that touches every area of managing a mid-market company. Independently and together, we've worked with CEOs of more than 2,000 mid-market companies in the United States, Europe, and Australia.

Part of our key findings in working with mid-market companies is that, while most CEOs and executives find value in the ideas and concepts presented in business books, few have the time or resources to synthesize those concepts and deploy them in the business to make tangible improvements. As such, we realized that taking the traditional course of presenting our findings in a book format would present only half a solution for many companies.

Because of our desire to create a complete solution, we took a different approach:

We developed the ShortTrack CEO book to present our findings to the general public, while at the same time creating a business management system based on the concepts — supported by a complete set of tools designed for mid-market companies to use in their day-to-day operations, to implement the concepts presented here.

This enables mid-market CEOs who want to implement the four concepts within their companies—or their specific ShortTrack—the freedom to use their own timeframe and tools, or to use the structure, timeframe, and tools of the business management system we created.

The complete business management system is available at www.ShortTrackCEO.com.

Ken

table of contents

the mysterious mid-market company

The chief executive officer—the top ranking executive of a company—is the company leader charged with creating the company's strategic vision, aligning the company internally and externally to that vision, and executing to make that vision a reality.

While most agree on the CEO's role in the company, there are vast differences between CEOs of different-sized companies: differences in their training and preparedness for their job; differences in the skills of the people they rely upon; differences in the resources they have available to get information they need to make decisions; differences in what worries them and occupies their mind space; and differences in how they approach executing their strategy.

In this book, we organize U.S. companies into three distinct categories based on their size, using the following designations:

Fortune 500 and enterprise
Companies over $100 million in revenue

Mid-market
Companies between $1 million and $100 million in revenue

Small business
Companies under $1 million in revenue

It's easy to envision companies in the top and bottom categories. The Fortune 500 is huge conglomerates with thousands of employees. The small businesses are a retail shop, a restaurant, a small services firm. The picture of a mid-market company is not as clear. We've selected this revenue band for mid-market companies to represent the general characteristics of the companies we've studied and worked with over the last 10 years.

Analysts disagree as to the exact criteria that define mid-market companies. Some say they're $100 million to $1 billion in revenue. Others say they're $10 million to $250 million in revenue. Their opinions often depend upon their industry, their training, and their perspective. Certainly there are companies over $1 million that operate like a small business instead of a mid-market company.

There are also $250 million companies operating like a mid-market company instead of an enterprise. The industry, the age of the company, and the funding source are all variables that contribute to whether a company at the low or high ends of the revenue band operates like a small business, a mid-market company, or an enterprise.

Based on our experience, we have found that the majority of the CEOs running companies between $1 million and $100 million in revenue encounter similar challenges and feel similar pressures that can be alleviated by the findings we're presenting in this book.

As of July 2010, there are 500 CEOs running Fortune 500 companies and another 32,000 running enterprises over $100 million in revenue, in the United States.* This comprises the enterprise group. There are 3,000,000 CEOs running mid-market companies from $1 million to $100 million in revenue and another 6,700,000 running small businesses under $1 million in revenue.

Our experience has shown us that a typical CEO of a company in each

* We'll refer to this category simply as the Fortune 500 in this book

3

category is different from CEOs in the other two categories. This assumption is fairly logical, and it's easy to understand that a Steve Jobs is quite different from Charlie Smith who owns the local hardware store.

Our focus is on the CEO who lives and works in the stratosphere between those of Steve Jobs and Charlie Smith; the 3,000,000 mid-market CEOs who are a hybrid of Steve Jobs and Charlie Smith.

Who is Studying the Mid-Market Company?

There are plenty of great business books written for Fortune 500 companies by CEOs and researchers (*Good to Great, Jack, Execution, The HP Way, Titan*). And there are plenty of great books written for small business owners (*The Art of the Start, The E-Myth Revisited, The Monk and the Riddle, Jumpstart Your Business Brain*). There are relatively few books, however, written specifically for and about mid-market companies.

Why?

It's an interesting question. Fortune 500 CEOs are in charge of multi-billion dollar companies, make eight figures per year, and interact with politicians, government officials, and celebrities. In fact, many of them are celebrities themselves. They're the focus of books, business school studies, biographies, and auto-biographies.

And most business books written by academics speak to big companies. This makes sense, since it's easier to research and study big companies because of the transparency of their financial information. Big companies are also typically better able to implement new ideas presented in business books, and many of the academics and researchers come from the same schools as the leaders of the companies they study—Harvard, Stanford, Wharton—and are connected through their alumni programs.

Small business owners are everyday people—your neighbors and friends—entrepreneurs who took a chance and went into business for themselves. It's difficult to start your own business, and extremely difficult to keep it going for more than five years. Starting a business is a dream of many—breaking away from the shackles of your job to become your own boss. The business section of any bookstore is always packed with stories, guides, and advice about how to start your own business in this or that industry. It's inspiring. It's sexy. In a free market economy, there will always be books about how to start a small business.

But the bookstores are conspicuously absent of stories, guides, or manuals for CEOs of mid-market companies: the $40 million electrical distributor in Waukegan, the $60 million trucking company in Wabash, or the $20 million pool manufacturer in Williamsport.

Over the last ten years we've worked with more than 2,000 CEOs of mid-market companies in the United States, Europe, and Australia. Mid-market companies have been our focus, and they're the focus of this book. We set out on this journey because we've been mid-market CEOs ourselves; we've worked with them and we've studied them. And what we've found is that they face challenges that are very different from those of Fortune 500 CEOs or small-business owners.

Most mid-market CEOs have a common set of struggles, but their struggles aren't addressed, and nor are solutions presented by the material in the marketplace that is geared toward the Fortune 500 or small business owners.

Our experience and research has enabled us to clarify and quantify the *intricacies* of how the mid-market CEO is different from the Fortune 500 CEO and the small business owner. As we've identified and learned about the differences over the years, we've worked to develop solutions for those mid-market CEOs and their leadership teams—who are the focus of this book.

two different journeys to the CEO role

Mid-market CEOs have a vastly different journey in their role, as compared to that of the Fortune 500 CEOs. Many started out as owners of successful small businesses that kept growing until they became mid-market companies. Others purchased a business and appointed themselves the CEO. A fair number of them have taken the reigns from a parent or a grandparent who founded the company.

Fortune 500 CEOs, not counting the select few like Larry Ellison or Bill Gates who founded their companies, were hired by sophisticated boards after a CEO succession process (Steve Jobs doesn't count because he was fired by the board in 1985 and then rehired 10 years later.)

Simply put, most Fortune 500 CEOs were hired by an independent board following a rigorous selection process. Most mid-market CEOs appointed themselves as the CEO or were given the role by a family member.

Their training is different, as well. Most Fortune 500 CEOs own graduate degrees from elite universities and have run different divisions of larger companies over a ten- to fifteen-year period. These divisions themselves are often double, triple, or quadruple the size of a large mid-market company. This exposes them to different challenges and builds broad and deep managerial and leadership skill sets. These CEOs-in-training are heavily groomed for the top spot by working directly with the existing CEO over a three- to five-year period.

Some mid-market CEOs have graduate degrees, and most have training in a specific field such as engineering, finance, accounting, or sales. They've learned their craft well; they've excelled at it, and eventually ended up with the top role in the company. But few have received substantial preparation, grooming, or training for their CEO role. And almost none is anywhere near as prepared for their CEO responsibilities as are their big company counterparts.

Competition for the jobs is different as well. The competition for Fortune 500 CEO roles is fierce—there are limited jobs and the rewards are high. Companies may deploy their CEO succession plan five years in advance of the CEO's scheduled retirement, giving them plenty of time to hone their search and to prepare and evaluate candidates.

On May 25, 2010, EMCOR Group, a U.S. based Fortune 500 company in mechanical and electrical construction, energy infrastructure, and facilities, announced the results of their CEO succession plan.

Example of a Fortune 500 CEO landing his role

EMCOR Group, Inc., a Fortune 500 leader in mechanical and electrical construction, energy infrastructure and facilities services, today announced that its Chairman and Chief Executive Officer, Frank T. MacInnis, age 63, will retire as Chief Executive Officer effective January 3, 2011, after serving as such for over 16 years. It is expected that Mr. MacInnis will continue to serve as non-executive Chairman of EMCOR's Board of Directors.

Mr. Anthony J. Guzzi, age 46, current EMCOR President and Chief Operating Officer, will succeed Mr. MacInnis as Chief Executive Officer. Mr. Guzzi was elected to the Board of Directors in December 2009, will remain a director of the Company, and will retain the title of President. As part of the Company's succession planning process, Mr. Guzzi was identified as a potential successor to Mr. MacInnis when he joined the Company in 2004 as President and Chief Operating Officer.

Stephen W. Bershad, Chair of the Board's Compensation and Personnel Committee, stated ..."Today's announcement ensures continued strong leadership for EMCOR. Tony Guzzi is a proven leader in the industry, ideally suited to succeed Frank as Chief Executive Officer and to guide EMCOR's growth in the years to come. Tony has played a key leadership role in the Company's transformation over the past five years. He has been instrumental in driving the Company's successful effort to diversify its revenue and profit base, and to enable it to prosper across economic cycles, as evidenced by the Company's excellent performance in the recent recession.

He has also played a critical role in leading

(continued)

9

(continued)

EMCOR's disciplined approach to project bidding, program management and cost controls, all of which have enabled the Company to weather the recent downturn in the market and be positioned to take advantage of the eventual rebound."

...

Mr. Guzzi stated, "I've learned a great deal from working closely with Frank for nearly six years, and I'm honored and very excited to take on this opportunity to lead EMCOR. EMCOR continues to benefit from our broad and diverse market exposure, as the initiatives we have undertaken have positioned us to capitalize on opportunities across our end markets. I look forward to leading the Company in the coming years and continuing our strategy for growth and success."

Prior to joining EMCOR Group, Mr. Guzzi held a variety of senior leadership positions at United Technologies and its subsidiary Carrier Corporation from 1997 to October 2004. Prior to joining United Technologies, Mr. Guzzi was an Engagement Manager at McKinsey & Company from 1993 to 1996.

From 1986 to 1991, he served in the U.S. Army as a Light Infantry Captain and is Ranger qualified. Mr. Guzzi received a B.S. in Civil Engineering and Economics from the United States Military Academy (West Point) in 1986. He received an M.B.A. from Harvard Business School.

The EMCOR example illustrates the depth of the training Mr. Guzzi has received for his CEO role: six years of close work with the current CEO; seven years of varied leadership roles at other companies, giving him exposure to many facets of business; the broad base of training—engineering, economics, a masters degree in business from Harvard; U.S. military experience; board experience; CFO experience; and his role as president of the company.

The fable on the next page, of a typical mid-market company CEO, illustrates the differences in the backgrounds of CEOs of the two groups. Bob Jones is a well-educated, well-trained engineer who is very good at what he does, but he's no longer an engineer building intricate computer systems—Bob is now a CEO of a $20 million company. He has seven well-defined years of engineering training, 20 years of experience designing and building aircraft monitoring systems, and zero years of CEO training.

Bob Jones is learning on the job, and he's no different from most of the 3,000,000 other mid-market CEOs in the United States.

The Impact of Training

This vast difference in training for the CEO role is the main reason that mid-market companies struggle to execute company strategy and the goals of the CEO, while the Fortune 500 companies thrive.

Multiple studies show that the key to elite performance in any field is training—a certain *type* of training and a certain *amount* of training.

In Malcolm Gladwell's best-seller *Outliers*, the author suggests (after studying people such as Bill Gates, Bill Joy, Eric Schmidt and Steve Jobs, among others) that achieving elite business performance results from a combination of three factors:

Example of a mid-market CEO landing his role

Bob Jones was a fabulous engineer. In school he studied physics, chemistry, geometry, and calculus. He mastered computer-assisted design and devoured engineering science and theory for an additional 4 years at MIT. He earned his masters in electrical engineering at Cal Tech and passed his state and professional board requirements to earn his license.

Bob worked for Raytheon for 20 years designing and building aircraft monitoring systems. He completed 3 weeks of ongoing training each year to keep his certifications intact. He became a department head, and was recognized as the most talented and well-trained engineer in the company. He knew his product inside and out, and realized that Raytheon was missing a market opportunity.

So Bob and a few of his direct reports quit Raytheon and spent 2 years building a different aircraft monitoring system. This one worked for commercial planes instead of military planes. Bob's close college buddy was a VP at Boeing, and after a product demonstration and two weeks of meetings, Bob landed a $20 million dollar contract with Boeing.

He is now the CEO of a mid-market company.

1. Being smart enough, which he states is having an IQ at 120 or above. Whether an IQ is 121 or 180 has no additional bearing on the business person's success.

2. Timing, or being in the right place at the right time, which means having an opportunity and taking advantage of it.

3. Practice or training—specifically, 10,000 hours of it. For a business person, this is roughly 5 years of full-time work or 10 years of part-time work.

In Geoff Colvin's best-seller *Talent Is Overrated*, he suggests that elite performance doesn't result from general experience, specific inborn abilities, or talent and memory; it results from deliberate practice— challenging training that improves the key areas of the discipline. He argues that deliberate practice is mentally demanding across all disciplines and can be effective when performed between one and five hours per day. This deliberate practice isn't fun, but as long as you have the basic natural skills to perform in your chosen field, it is the single *differentiator* between average performers and elite performers.

This vast difference in training between the enterprise and mid-market CEO is the first and primary differentiator between the two. Most Fortune 500 CEOs have had five to ten years of grooming and training for their CEO role. Most of the mid-market CEOs were trained in something *other* than being a CEO.

And it directly contributes to their struggles.

Key Takeaway

Most CEOs of mid-market companies have a deep understanding of their product/service, and extensive training and experience in a specific business area, but rarely have benefit of the depth and breadth of the CEO training received by a Fortune 500 CEO. Fortune 500 CEOs are hired by sophisticated boards after lengthy hiring processes. Most mid-market CEOs arrive at their role by self-appointment (either by starting or purchasing a business) or by being handed the position from a family member.

delegation, information, and decision making on the job

When Mr. Guzzi and Mr. Jones assume their roles, they'll both take ownership of the company leadership, strategy, and vision. This is something Fortune 500 and mid-market company CEOs have in common.

But the balance of the on-the-job activities will differ, often substantially. Mr. Guzzi will manage a group of highly-skilled and trained c-level executives, vice presidents, and general managers (there were 17 listed on www.emcorgroup.com as of July 2010). He'll work with analysts, the EMCOR board, the media, the government, partners, and key customers. His role, after setting the vision and strategy, is primarily to coordinate activities at a very high level and rely upon his other executives to manage their business areas and execute his strategy.

Mr. Jones will manage a small group of financial, technical, and operational executives. The nature of his business doesn't justify bringing aboard a VP of Sales yet, but this is a bit atypical, and he will do so once he starts expanding. Mr. Jones will operate in what looks like a hybrid role—a mixture of Fortune 500 CEO activities and entrepreneurial activities that are the purview of the small business owner. He'll still have a heavy focus on operations as they build their monitoring systems, as it would be difficult for him to turn away from the work he's done so well for so many years.

He'll also spend time monitoring cash flow and handling employee issues, but his first hires will be a VP of Finance and an HR manager to take these responsibilities off his plate. This is common amongst mid-market CEOs.

Another difference between the Fortune 500 and mid-market CEO results from the background of the people they rely upon. The Fortune 500 CEO's key executive team often have similar skills and background as the CEO

F500 example of time breakdown

HOW JEFF IMMELDT, CEO OF GE, ALLOCATES HIS TIME:

15% with customers

30% on people, teaching or coaching

10% on governance (working with the board & meeting with investors)

45% on the "plumbing" of the company, i.e. operating reviews and strategy sessions

Mid-market example of time breakdown

HOW TYPICAL MID-MARKET CEOS ALLOCATE THEIR TIME:

43% with customers

22% on people, teaching or coaching

2% on governance

33% operations and strategy

had when he was rising through the ranks. They have graduate degrees from elite schools and ten to fifteen years of experience managing different facets of the business, with many having P&L responsibility for divisions far exceeding $100 million in revenue.

The mid-market CEO has a far smaller stable of executives. While an $80 million company will have more key executives than an $8 million company, the average mid-market company CEO has a CFO or financial executive, a VP of Sales, one or two operational executives, and two or three key managers.

And the Fortune 500 CEOs and mid-market CEOs are thinking about different things.

Fortune 500 CEOs' mind space is occupied by	Mid-market CEOs' mind space is occupied by
1. Shareholders	1. Customers
2. Managing committees	2. Employees
3. Stock price	3. Cash flow
4. Brand	4. Sales
5. Political appointments	5. Family employees
6. Cashout	6. Individual net worth

Another obvious difference between the two is the amount of resources at their disposal. Billion dollar companies have the budgets—and sometimes almost unlimited ability—to hire headcount and consultants and to acquire the information they need during their course of business. Mid-market companies have limited budgets and limited financial resources.

These differences illustrate how the mid-market CEO operates differently from his Fortune 500 counterpart. In comparing the two, the deck is definitely stacked against mid-market CEOs; they have lower amounts of intellectual capital at their disposal, fewer financial resources, less training, and a different mindset than that of Fortune 500 CEOs.

Delegation

The prior training of a mid-market CEO, whether it's in finance, engineering, or sales, affects how they decide what business areas to delegate and what business areas to own. Most mid-market CEOs immediately give away areas outside their expertise—most commonly sales management, human resources, and hiring. These are critical areas of the business, and the smaller the company, the less training and skill the person handling them is likely to have.

When mid-market CEOs delegate areas within their own expertise, (for example, when a financially-trained CEO hires a CFO), they often tend to micromanage the executive they've placed in charge of the area. When things get tough, or the company enters a crisis, this is exacerbated. The spirit of the mid-market CEO is to roll up his sleeves and dive into operations (most often his area of expertise). He is most comfortable being "one of the team" in a crisis situation. This typically has a negative effect, undermining the credibility of the executive in charge of the area.

Fortune 500 CEOs rarely dig deep into business areas they've delegated. They'll work with executives to adjust their strategy to handle the crises and hold the executives accountable for implementing a new course of action.

The common end result is that most mid-market CEOs delegate functions that they should own or still manage with oversight, and work in areas that they should delegate. It's a natural result of their previous training, the path that led them to the job, and their desire to improve the company. We're not suggesting that mid-market CEOs become HR directors and sales managers; we're suggesting that giving away complete ownership of these functions contributes to the typical struggles of mid-market companies.

Decision Making

When it comes to decision making, any leader will be forced to make decisions with imperfect information. In the best-selling fable *The Five Temptations of a CEO* by Patrick Lencioni, the author suggests that too many CEOs hold off on making decisions because of their fear of being wrong. He further suggests that CEOs should choose clarity over certainty, and making a decision with imperfect information is good, as long as the CEO owns up to it, even if the decision turns out to be wrong.

Our experience has shown that there's a substantial difference in the information that Fortune 500 CEOs rely upon compared to what the mid-market CEOs have to rely upon when making key decisions. Fortune 500 CEOs typically have a talented executive team and the budget to obtain the resources and information they need, to support or refute important business decisions. In fact, their c-level executives and vice-presidents have it as well.

Since mid-market CEOs have fewer resources—training and intellectual capital, and the budget to obtain it—they're forced to make decisions with far less clarity than the Fortune 500 CEO. It's quite common for mid-market CEOs to use their gut instinct for important decisions instead of relying on relevant information that will confirm or refute their intuition.

While most mid-market CEOs have good gut instinct (that has substantially contributed to their success), many make far too many important decisions on gut instinct alone. This can occur for any of the following reasons:

- They don't have the resources or ability to obtain the information they need to achieve clarity.

- They're relying upon the wrong information.

- They don't know that the information is available.

Having good intuition is an important trait for a CEO, but sometimes complexities in business, such as slopes of supply and demand curves, cash flow velocity, quality of revenue, and profitability ratings can foil good intuition. Or, in many instances, the CEO's intuition might be correct, but a lower-level manager without the same degree of gut instinct might be handling the decision. As strong as your intuition may be, it's important to support it with quality information to confirm or refute your instincts. This works not to provide certainty, but to provide *clarity*, as Patrick Lencioni suggests, to enable you to make better decisions throughout the year.

Fortune 500 CEOs and executives understand this and use information to support their key decisions that affect their company's performance.

Most of the information that mid-market CEOs need is within their reach; they just need to know how to find it.

Key Takeaway

Mid-market CEOs approach their roles differently from Fortune 500 CEOs, relying more upon gut-instinct to make decisions, instead of relying often upon relevant data to confirm or refute their instinct.

execution
of
your
strategy

Are there common reasons that companies of *all* categories struggle—small businesses, mid-market, and Fortune 500? Are there commonalities between the challenges encountered by CEOs in companies within each category?

Our assumptions about the common struggles of companies of all sizes are anecdotal, taken from our business experience and observations, and staying abreast of business thinking by consistently studying the works of thought-leaders around the globe.

Based on that experience, we found that the main business challenges occupying CEOs' mind space fall into three areas:

People
How to get the right people aboard and how to best motivate and lead them

Growth and competition
How to get bigger and win market share

Execution
How to get things done

Most mid-market CEOs understand the importance of leadership and vision and have successfully endeavored to enhance their skills in these areas over the years. But the nature of the mid-market company— limited financial resources, limited intellectual capital, and a heavy focus on tactical day-to-day activities—makes these leadership skills less impactful than they would be at a Fortune 500 company, where the executive team and managers have a greater ability to apply high-level concepts in their day-to-day operations.

In most mid-market companies, effective leadership can motivate the executive team and managers to work harder, but it's uncommon for them to work on new things that will improve the performance of the business. Most of the time they simply put more energy into *working on the same things*, which rarely changes long-term business results.

Strategy Isn't the Problem

In our work with more than 2,000 mid-market CEOs, we've never once heard a CEO utter, "I don't have a strategy." All CEOs have a strategy. Most CEO strategies are very good. You don't get to the top spot of any corporation, regardless of your path to it, without a sharp mind and strategic-thinking ability.

We've found that the common struggle of most mid-market CEOs is execution—not execution of low-level tactics such as manufacturing processes, selling skills, or financial reporting—we're talking about execution of company strategy at the highest level. This is personal and emotional to the mid-market CEO—the feeling that *We're struggling because the team can't execute my strategy.*

◀◀ We're struggling because the team can't execute my strategy.

In our experience, the first two challenges on our list—how best to attract, motivate, and lead the right people, and how to get bigger and grow market share—are each part of our third, more general challenge of executing a mid-market CEO's overall strategy. For this reason, we'll address all three challenges here, in our discussion on execution of strategy.

CEOs Are Concerned About Execution

Surveys show that execution is one of the top worries of most CEOs.

From The Conference Board CEO Challenge 2010 Top 10 Challenges Paper

CEO Challenge 2010
Top 10 Challenges

United States Top 10
(N = 207)
Cite challenge as being of Relative Ranking "greatest concern in the coming year"

2008	2009	Challenge	2009	2008
1	1	Excellence in execution	47.3%	55.6%
3	2	Sustained and steady top-line growth	44.6	54.1
2	3	Consistent execution of strategy by top management	39.8	54.5
5	4	Customer loyalty/retention	38.2	40.4
12	5	Profit growth	30.9	26.5
19	6	Government regulation	29.7	13.3

2008	2009	Challenge	2009	2008
15	7	Corporate reputation for quality products/services	24.6	17.2
4	8	Speed, flexibility, adaptability to change	20.3	42.9
14	9	Stimulating innovation/creativity/ enabling entrepreneurship	19.0	20.4
28	10	Cash management	17.5	9.3

The *CEO Challenge 2010* survey involved U.S. CEOs across all revenue categories. The concerns shared by CEOs about execution—their companies' ability to get things done—are not new. The best-seller *Execution* by Larry Bossidy, former Chairman of Honeywell International, and Ram Charan, a highly sought-after consultant for Fortune 500 CEOs and executive teams, articulated company leaders' concerns about execution back in 2002. Eight years later, execution still tops the mind space of U.S. CEOs.

The premise of *Execution* is that execution is the missing link between aspirations and results, and that, to be successful, strategies must take into account the organization's ability to execute.

The authors argue that company leaders are able to execute well by aligning three processes in a company: the strategy process, the people process, and the operations process.

When companies don't link these three core processes together, the companies rarely perform well. The book contains details of both successful and unsuccessful execution at corporations such as Dell, Johnson & Johnson, and Xerox, along with these pearls of execution wisdom for leaders:

1. Know your people and your business.

2. Insist on realism.

3. Set clear goals and priorities.

4. Follow through.

5. Reward the doers.

6. Expand people's capabilities through coaching.

7. Know yourself.

Reviews of the book on Amazon.com typically fall into two categories: those by readers who love the examples and high-level concepts presented in the book, and endeavor to apply them at their own companies; and those by disappointed readers who felt it was too high-level and elementary, focusing far too much on corporate "war stories" instead of giving valuable advice on *how* to execute better.

If we had to guess, we'd bet the supporters are mainly managers and executives of enterprise companies—those who have the time and resources to determine how to apply the high-level concepts presented in the book at their own companies.

The Fortune 500 embrace books that present high-level business concepts because they have armies of MBAs and consultants who are paid to determine how to most effectively apply those concepts to the problem areas of their businesses. Mid-market companies have limited bandwidth and struggle to apply general business concepts at their companies because:

- It's difficult for managers to break away from the chaos of day-to-day business to make impactful changes that improve execution of strategy.

- They don't have sufficient budget or intellectual capital (i.e., people with the training and experience to create and manage projects of this nature) to apply general concepts to their business.

Because they have the ability and resources to improve their business by applying general concepts, we would argue that Fortune 500 companies tend to execute better than mid-market companies do. While this argument is anecdotal, as we haven't conducted a research study comparing performance of the two groups (like the work of Jim Collins and Jerry Porras, as presented in their book *Built to Last*), we base our assertion on evidence that comes from thousands of mid-market CEOs we've worked with—CEOs who struggle every day to get their teams to execute their strategy, having seen no growth in five years, no bottom-line improvements, and little additional value created. And most importantly, they're not getting closer to their personal end goal.

Mid-Market CEOs Are Seeking Specific Solutions

Mid-market CEOs haven't asked us for general solutions. These savvy leaders already know the general things they need to do to improve and execute their strategy: increase sales, improve operational efficiency, and reduce costs.

Mid-market CEOs have asked us for *specific* solutions—guidance on what to do and how to do it, day-in and day-out. It's been our focus for the last ten years, as we've built a framework of concepts tying together the high-level aspects of running any business—shifting the mid-market CEO from the hybrid role of chief executive officer and small business owner, into a role that mirrors that of the Fortune 500 CEO—but in a format that mid-market CEOs can manage and use with their teams.

We've organized our findings into four specific concepts that start with simple ideas, and then drill down to the activities that improve performance of mid-market companies. While these are high-level concepts, they are ideas and activities that, when embraced and properly implemented, address the common elements that cause mid-market executive teams to struggle to execute the strategy and personal goals of their CEO.

1. Your CFO is not giving you all the numbers you need to confirm your everyday decisions.

2. You have the ability to take the guesswork out of managing your people.

3. You must win mind share to influence your market.

4. Your team must be able to clearly articulate your purpose and your vision.

The next four chapters outline each concept in detail and recommend activities to easily implement them in your day-to-day workflow.

concept 1:

your CFO is not giving you all the numbers you need to confirm your everyday decisions.

Overview

It's not difficult to quantify your basic operational results from numbers on standard financial statements: profit and loss, cash flow, assets, liabilities, and equity.

Finance executives and accountants complete years of training and master a defined set of requirements to produce these types of traditional statements and reports. They're a necessity—for the U.S. government, banks, vendors, and investors.

Mid-market CEOs pay attention to these numbers and, for most, they're the numbers they use to gauge performance. But what do these numbers really tell us? Do these standard financial statements truly measure the value our operations are generating? Can we use them in real time to confirm or refute our instincts, while making the hundreds of operational decisions each month that impact our performance?

If your team were to ask you any of the questions below, how long would it take to respond with a solid answer supported by firm dollar amounts?

- If we increase our prices 3%, will our revenue go up or down? What about our profits?

- What happens to our company value if we enter this new market?

- If we offer a 5% discount to our suppliers to pay net 10, does that improve the value of our company?

- Our input prices are rising. Should we lock in a fixed price? How can we quantify the impact on our business if we don't do this, and prices keep increasing?

- Can we afford this new equipment?

- Should we lower our prices to sell more and increase our revenue?

- How is this strategic investment affecting our financial performance?

- How are our staff costs tracking against revenue generation, and what impact will a 2% increase in productivity have on our cash flow and return?

To get answers, do you refer to your P&L, your balance sheet, or your cash flow statement?

Of course you don't. Standard financial statements don't deliver answers to these questions. But savvy finance people learned long ago that there are plenty of numbers that can be extracted from these financial statements—hidden from plain view, but accessible—that can deliver the answers to these types of questions.

Fortune 500 financial executives understand this. Their teams produce the standard numbers required for public markets—the balance sheet, the profit and loss statements, and the cash flow statements—but most use an even deeper set of numbers to truly understand their strengths and weaknesses, their past performance, and the *consequences* of their future operational decisions. These include numbers like TBR, CFROI, RONA, EVA, ROCE and EROCE.

Few mid-market CEOs reference these types of numbers. They all have access to them but most don't use them because of a perception that they are overly-complicated. It's common for mid-market CEOs without a traditional finance and accounting background to feel that their CFO is speaking one language, while the CEO and the rest of the executive team are speaking another—business speak versus finance speak. There's nothing wrong with finance speak; it simply isn't very useful to most executives who need numerical information to support or refute decisions that they need to make *today*, in real time.

We call these the *hidden numbers*: They're the numbers that exist between the P&L and the balance sheet, hidden from plain view if you're using only a traditional financial statement. They're immensely valuable to the executives that seek them out and use them to support their daily business decisions.

> ◀◀ We call these the *hidden numbers*: They're the numbers that exist between the P&L and the balance sheet, hidden from plain view...

By viewing these hidden numbers, mid-market CEOs can understand—in real time—how operational changes will affect *future* performance resulting from:

- Pricing changes

- Volume changes

- Operational changes that affect direct and indirect costs

- Changes to receivables, payables, and inventory

- Changes to fixed assets

- Strategic investments

What about the mid-market CEO who wants to understand how he's performing relative to his competitors and peers? Mid-market CEOs don't have public markets to measure how well they're doing and what their company is worth. The unfortunate reality is that the standard numbers most mid-market CEOs rely on quantify only past operational performance and give little intelligence on:

- How much value they're creating

- How well they're performing against their competition

- How well they're performing against their peers

- How strong their future will be

Hidden numbers can deliver answers to all these questions. To uncover these hidden numbers and gain the same real-time information that Fortune 500 executives use, you may need to change the way you approach three specific operational activities that we examine here.

Activity #1: Budgeting and Forecasting

How frequently do you budget? How often do you update your financial forecast?

Budgeting and forecasting is the first operational area to address in order to find more meaningful numbers to confirm your everyday decisions.

There are three common methods companies use to measure profit and loss results:

1. **Year-to-date**

2. **Trailing twelve months**

3. **24 month rolling**

Year-to-Date (YTD)

Year-to-date measurement is normally accompanied by annual budgeting. It is the most common but least effective method. Here's how it works:

> Companies create an annual forecast during the yearly budgeting process. After each month concludes, they record their results and track their progress toward the original forecast. When the year concludes, management spends precious time and energy trying to explain variances that resulted because circumstances changed after the budget had already been set in stone.

While this traditional process is better than not budgeting at all, it has minimal value.

The main reason it's an ineffective tool to assist with current business decisions is that it displays past information that sheds little light on current and future business conditions. Some companies have even given up on the process entirely, not wanting to waste time creating projections that they might very well never live up to anyway.

> ▌▌ While this traditional process is better than not budgeting at all, it has minimal value.

Forecasting is never 100% accurate—it's simply a prediction of the future at a given point in time. Companies that predict their future 12 months out, and never update it as each month progresses, are akin to a driver on the road who stares at a spot 120 yards ahead, and continues to stare at it until he hits that spot. No driver would do that—one of the first lessons in driver's education is to keep your field of vision consistently forward.

The same concept applies to business. Conditions are changing constantly, providing new information that makes the original estimates less and less accurate with each passing month. Change is constant, but YTD forecasting doesn't factor change into the equation.

Trailing Twelve Months (TTM)

An increasingly popular method of measuring profit and loss is called Trailing Twelve Months (TTM). TTM is a moving measurement that includes the most recent twelve months of financial statements instead of an aggregate result from a given period of time (such as a month, a quarter, or a year.)

TTM is powerful because it removes the impact of seasonality. When you chart your TTM results each month, you see a moving average of past performance that clearly highlights the trends of your business performance.

24 Month Rolling (24MR)

The 24 month rolling method (24MR) incorporates the two concepts addressed in the previous examples:

1. Using a moving average of past performance

2. Keeping the field of vision consistently forward

24MR incorporates TTM and includes 12 months of projections, all in one statement, to present an even clearer picture of business performance—past, present, and future.

The 24MR method is more powerful than TTM because it keeps your field of vision 12 months ahead at all times, rather than focused on just the current date.

◀◀ The 24MR method keeps your field of vision 12 months ahead at all times, rather than focused on just the current date.

To create a 24 month rolling forecast for any financial statement, add 12 months of predictions to each line item in your TTM. The resulting collation of 24 months of data is a blend of your TTM history and a prediction of the next 12 months.

It's important to ensure that someone within the company takes ownership of this process. The common assumption is that, because forecasting is numerical, the CFO should own the process. But before accepting this kind of arrangement just because that's how it's always been in the past, ask yourself this question:

Who in your business is best qualified to predict and influence the future?

The most common answers to this question are: CEO, COO, Sales Manager, or Operations Manager, but rarely is it the CFO. So is the CFO really the best person to own your documented vision of the future? While the CFO will be integral to the process, a better result may be achieved if the whole executive team gets involved, with the CEO at the helm.

At the close of each month, complete the 3 following steps:

1. Change the closing month's forecast to actual results.

2. Ask your team two simple but powerful questions: "What information has come to light in the last 30 days that changes our view of the future?" And, based on that conversation, "How do we need to change our behavior, and what actions do we need to instigate now, to accommodate and influence the future?" Take the answer to these two questions and update the line items of the future 11 months' forecast.

3. Now extend the forecast to include the month one year beyond the month just closed—and insert predictions for each line item.

Transition from YTD to 24MR

Step 2 enables you to update previous forecasts 11 times (once a month) before recording actual results. This process allows for continual updating and improvement of the 12 month forecast, reducing guesswork to project a more-certain result. When blended with the historical results of your TTM, a more powerful set of numbers appears, to illuminate how the business is performing.

The key to Step 2 is to keep the conversation at the operational level for as long as possible before drilling down to numerical implications.

This keeps the forecasting in the hands of the business people who are closest to the information that impacts the financial forecast. Typical operational questions can be:

- What is our proposed pricing strategy going forward?

- Will foreign exchange rates affect us?

- What is happening to our input prices, e.g., steel /crude oil / people?

- Are there new competitors in the market?

- Are we running new marketing campaigns?

- Have projects slipped backward or come forward?

- Are we opening new markets?

- Are we shifting product focus?

- Are we bringing aboard new people?

- Is our product mix changing?

❝ The key to Step 2 is to keep the conversation at the operational level for as long as possible before drilling down to numerical implications.

Resistance to 24MR

Is there resistance to 24MR in mid-market companies? Of course there is. CFOs typically deliver the most resistance, using the argument, "We've used the standard method of tracking performance for years. Why do we need all this additional detail?" The main reason for this resistance is that CFOs and financial people have completed years of standardized training and this new protocol might feel like a paradigm shift.

After years or decades of operating in a particular way, a change like this— something that wasn't part of the CPA or MBA curriculum—rocks the boat and can feel like a challenge to their authority. It's rare that a CFO at a mid-market level embraces this type of change without some persuasion.

Operational people also resist moving to 24MR because, on the surface, it appears that they'll have to complete the painful budgeting process *each month* instead of only once a year. That's 12 times the pain!

There's no argument that asking your team at the end of each month to consider the question, "What information has come to light in the last 30 days that changes our view of the future," and then asking them to update future projections, may create additional monthly work. But the reality is that, once the initial learning curve has been overcome, this process makes budgeting easier and more accurate, and spreads it out over 12 months, instead of compacting it into a single, exhaustive period once a year.

▲▲ What information has come to light in the last 30 days that changes our view of the future?

Furthermore, if this process does nothing but encourage CEOs to ask their key executives this critical question, it will still deliver significant value; arguably, this is the most crucial question the CEO should be asking, regardless of the forecasting culture.

The 24MR process also takes the pressure and pain off the once-a-year budgeting, and offsets the "hit-the-target" mentality. Part of the reason once-a-year budgeting is so painful is that it's eminently difficult—like throwing darts at a board—and too much pressure is placed on managers to prove that their number is accurate. Many managers' performance is tied to meeting or exceeding what ultimately boils down to deliberate guesswork.

The key issue with 24MR is not whether the forecast is correct or incorrect; the key issue is to encourage the CEO to review the team's best estimate for the future using the most reliable knowledge currently available and, if they are not happy with forecasted trends for the next 12 months, to act accordingly. Think of this as having the keys to a time machine that can carry you 12 months into the future and allow you to look back to the current date. If you do not like what you see, get back into the time machine, return to the current date, and take actions that will change the future.

Here are some other common reasons for resistance, along with the reality:

Resistance	Reality
Crystal ball / ability to read the future.	Take the pressure off your team to get their 12 month forecast right. They're going to get it wrong.
This is "moving the goal posts."	The goal posts are not moving; what's moving is your understanding of reality.
We have once-a-year transactions.	As long as they are done the same month each year (which is standard), once-a-year transactions will have no impact on 24MR.
Board approval of the budget.	This does not replace Board approval–this is the internal management process. But after seeing it in action, the Board will probably prefer to see this, rather than an out-of-date budget.
This will be more work, not less.	Initially it may be more work, but soon after implementing 24MR, most companies realize that the additional time is time well spent understanding and influencing the future.
People don't like budgeting.	True – don't use the word budgeting!
Monthly data is not ready by month's end.	Hire a better bookkeeper.
Processing items like depreciation each month is difficult.	Process once a year if you want – but in the same month every year.
My accounting system will not handle this.	This won't be handled in the accounting system.
How do I fit this into my already-crowded management agenda?	Put it at the top.

Resistance is common because new procedures require change and additional work on the front end. But once 24MR is implemented, your team will embrace the additional value it provides. More importantly, it will enable them to better execute company strategy.

So what is a common response of mid-market CEOs after implementing 24MR forecasting? Usually, it's along the lines of, "This is blindingly obvious—why didn't my financial people tell me about this before?"

Key Takeaway

Once-a-year budgeting and performance recording is out-of-date and provides minimal value. Expand your view to get a clearer, more accurate and more powerful picture of your business performance. All executives need to participate in this process–not just the CFO.

Activity #2: Strategic Investment Management

Who is in charge of your strategic investments? Who is responsible for managing and tracking their phases and their progress, and for measuring results and ensuring that they don't drastically damage the company? Do you have a protocol for managing their performance?

In many mid-market companies, no single person owns this responsibility. In other companies, it may be a group of executives. And most businesses do not have a formal process for evaluating and managing strategic investments.

For discussion purposes, let's call any strategic decision to spend money today for a benefit tomorrow a J Curve investment, or simply a *J Curve*. J Curves create short term financial loss with the intention of recovering the investment in the future, and overriding it with long term strategic gains.

Every business has J Curves. Here are some examples:

- Adding a new product line

- Accessing a new market

- Making a new staff hire

- Purchasing new equipment

- Opening a new location

- Moving manufacturing overseas

- Investing in R&D

- Acquiring competitors

Mid-market CEOs and their leadership teams intuitively understand when they're taking on J Curves. But it's rare for a mid-market company to measure and track either the performance of the J Curve as an independent entity, or its impact on the business as a whole. Should they, you ask?

Absolutely.

The process of identifying, prioritizing, and managing J Curves is the most important determinant of entrepreneurial success.

> " The process of identifying, prioritizing, and managing J Curves is the most important determinant of entrepreneurial success.

Rolls-Royce Declares Bankruptcy from Too Many J Curves

Rolls-Royce, a company known for engineering and quality, declared bankruptcy in 1971, 65 years after its founding. Much of the publicity surrounding the bankruptcy centered on the technical problems of the RB-211 jet engine, which eventually became one of the most popular jet engines in the world over the next 10 years.

To keep the weight of the engine down, Rolls-Royce engineers used lightweight carbon fibers for the fan blades, which shattered when hail or birds were sucked into the 7 ft fans. Deadlines were missed and production costs skyrocketed—common occurrences with J Curve investments.

But the engine's problems didn't cause the bankruptcy—for years Rolls-Royce had been committing itself to too many costly development projects simultaneously. At the time of the collapse, almost 40% of its employees were working on engines that were not yet profitable. Rolls-Royce collapsed because of too many J Curves at one time.

J Curve Framework

The first step in creating a J Curve management process is understanding the three phases of the J Curve, and understanding how your behavior will vary, depending on the stage you are in, whether it's:

1. Investment

2. Catch Up

3. Blue Sky

It's important for mid-market CEOs to understand how many J Curves they're currently undertaking and the status of each, because J Curves cost more than just the short-term drain on cash flow, return, and profit; they absorb substantial "executive head-space" and opportunity cost. Having no J Curves is bad; having too many J Curves at once can sink a booming company as shown in the Rolls-Royce example.

J Curves - 3 Phases

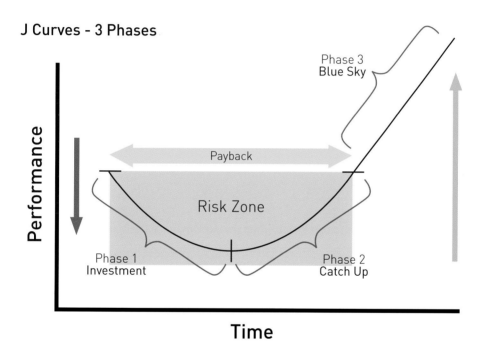

Rules for Managing J Curves

1. Measure and manage depth and breadth of the valley

Be prepared for the valley to be deeper and wider than anticipated. Encourage discussion about costs, and create an environment where new ideas are welcomed.

2. Do NOT become emotionally connected to a J Curve

Watch out for ski slopes, and emotional arguments to keep them going. Examples are sunken costs and people management.

3. Do NOT take on too many macro J Curves at once

Identify, prioritize, and stagger J Curves. Understand how many your company can handle at one time. Understand "aggressive" versus "passive" introduction, and ask two questions when considering any new J Curve: Will it benefit the business? Is now the right time?

4. Create and manage a plan to quickly move from Phase 1 to Phase 3

Focus on the critical transition between the innovator and the implementer by using clear communication, documentation, and procedures. And beware of innovators who will not let go of their baby!

5. Establish a J Curve register

The register will track the number of J Curves active in the business. Maintain the register in a spreadsheet, and update it every 30 days. The register isn't a project management system; it's a higher level view of all strategic investments in the business.

Other Considerations with J Curves

It's still important to monitor J Curves as they progress along the curve. J Curves that have reached Phase 3 can slip back to Phase 2, and those that have reached Phase 2 can slip back to Phase 1 (these are called "W Curves.")

J Curves can also be broken down into "macro" and "micro" J Curves. If you have both types, consider keeping a company-wide macro register that you manage yourself, and have your divisional managers maintain their own micro registers.

Key Takeaway

You must track and manage your J Curve investments with the utmost detail to understand:

1. How many J Curves you're undertaking

2. How each J Curve is progressing

3. When a J Curve should be abandoned

4. How well your core business is performing

Accomplish this by creating a J Curve register and evaluating each J Curve every 90 days.

Activity #3: Operational Decision Making

Using 24MR forecasting and a J Curve register will yield some very important numbers outside those rendered by standard financial statements, to help confirm some key business decisions. But what about some of the operational questions we posed at the beginning of this chapter, such as:

- If we change our prices to x, will our revenue go up or down? What about our profits?

- What happens to our company value if we enter this new market?

- Should we take a discount and pay early? Should we offer one?

You won't find answers to these questions in your standard financial statements, in your 24 month rolling forecast, or in your J Curve register. Most mid-market CEOs and their leadership teams use intuition to answer these questions. And often, their intuition is correct.

> *If I knew I could be right in 51% of my decisions, I'd make a lot of decisions.*
>
> *- Henry Ford*

But sometimes complexities in business, such as slopes of supply and demand curves, cash flow velocity, quality of revenue, and profitability ratings can foil good intuition. Or, in many instances, the CEO's intuition might be correct, but a lower-level manager without the same degree of "gut instinct" might be handling the decision.

> " The CEO's intuition might be correct, but a lower-level manager without the same level of "gut instinct" might be handling the decision.

As strong as your intuition may be, it's important to support it with a mathematical framework. The finance teams of Fortune 500 companies understand this and use their financial prowess to create and use a multitude of modeling tools to better understand the results of the decisions they're faced with—to confirm or refute their intuition. This is commonplace in big companies, but rare in mid-market companies.

The enterprise software packages commonly used by the Fortune 500 contain these types of sophisticated modeling tools. Advances in data mining software and business intelligence software in the last 5 to 10 years have conditioned top managers in big companies to consult the results of diverse financial modeling before making key decisions affecting their numerical performance.

Has this type of modeling software reached mid-market companies at a price and in a format that works for them?

Not yet.

Business intelligence and enterprise software packages, such as Oracle's Hyperion, IBM's Cognos, and SAP's Business Objects, run six to seven figures in cost. The market still is not mature, and it will take years (if ever) to see if these types of complex offerings can be delivered in smaller scale and at lower cost for mid-market companies to consume.

That leaves a single solution for mid-market companies:

- Build your own models

We're not suggesting that you become a software producer, but what we are suggesting is that most mid-market companies can afford to build *SOME* type of financial modeling tools that will deliver key information to confirm or refute important decisions and support intuition.

Examples of Modeling

Financial modeling delivers the real-time information you need for daily operational decisions. To determine what type of modeling to create, the first step is to decide what type of decisions you'd like to confirm. Here are some examples of what modeling can deliver:

- Impact of price changes

- Impact of volume changes

- Impact of changes in variable costs

- Impact of changes in fixed costs

- Impact of changes in inventory

- Impact of changes in accounts receivable

- Impact of changes in accounts payable

- Impact of changes in capital deployment

Microsoft Excel is a very powerful program, and Excel-based models can vary from simple to very complex. To build your own models, you need someone who can define what type of results they'd like to see, and an Excel expert to build them. If you don't have the experience in-house, there are plenty of consultants around the world who can build intricate Excel financial models for you. And with the global economy and easy access to talented financial and software people around the world, most mid-market companies should be able to fit some type of project within their budget.

The key is to start simple and begin using modeling tools. You can get more complex over time. And if you don't want to take on the responsibility of building them yourself, you should be able to find a talented consultant who has already built models that are ready for use.

The more of these models that you use, the closer you come to having the ability to confirm, before every operational decision, the answer to two simple questions:

1. Should we do this (i.e., will it improve our performance?)

2. Can we do this (i.e., can we afford it?)

Key Takeaway

Begin using financial modeling tools to confirm or refute decisions involving numbers. There's no reason to rely solely on your intuition for all these types of decisions. The Fortune 500 use them frequently. Using financial modeling improves the number of correct decisions you and your team make throughout the year—which improves your execution of company strategy.

Optional Activity: Measuring Your Performance as the CEO

How do you measure your performance each year as a CEO? Are you able to measure it against the performance of your competition? Against that of your peers?

Public company CEOs can easily get a real-time independent evaluation of their performance by taking a look at their stock price. This tells them very clearly how well they're performing relative to their past performance, to their competition, to their peers, and to market expectation itself.

Private company CEOs don't have public markets to measure how well they're performing and what their company is worth. The unfortunate reality is that the standard numbers most mid-market CEOs rely upon quantify only *past* operational performance and give little intelligence on:

- How much value they're creating

- How well they're performing against their competition

- How well they're performing against their peers

Other than comparing company revenue, number of employees, or the size of their houses, cars, boats, or other toys, how do CEOs of mid-market companies obtain this information? For most, they need to bring in independent experts: bankers, analysts, or financial consultants with sophisticated performance-modeling tools.

Fortune 500 financial executives have been using these types of tools for over 70 years. Their teams produce the standard numbers required for public markets, but most use an even deeper set of numbers to gain a true understanding of their strengths, their weaknesses, and their performance, with numbers like TBR, CFROI, RONA, EVA, ROCE and EROCE.

These are more complex than simple ROI calculations and are most valuable when they are used to facilitate a strategic and operational conversation about changing the future.

Calculations do not change businesses; influence and action do. And we've encountered many mid-market CEOs who make dramatic changes to their company after digging deeper to gain a true understanding of their performance.

Going the Extra Mile

Using these types of sophisticated tools is an optional part of Concept #1: *Your CFO is not giving you all the numbers you need to confirm your everyday decisions.*

It's deeper and more complex than the three main activities supporting the concept, but for those mid-market CEOs who truly desire to measure their performance and understand exactly how much value they're creating, this is a way to accomplish it.

Key Takeaway

To get a true measurement of your performance as a CEO, your bottom-line skill on the job, and your ability to create value for your company, you need to bring in experts to deploy sophisticated financial performance measurement tools.

Concept Summary
Your CFO is not giving you all the numbers you need to confirm your everyday decisions.

What to *unlearn*:
Using static, once-a-year budgeting; using static financial statements to measure performance; using intuition to track strategic investments; relying on intuition instead of financial modeling to confirm decisions involving measurable numbers; using traditional financial statements to measure your performance.

What to *learn*:
Rolling forecasting; the J Curve register; financial models to get real-time answers as to whether your operational decisions are correct–to confirm your instinct.

How the Fortune 500 approach it:
By using sophisticated financial modeling tools and ratios to forecast, support decisions, track investments, and measure performance.

concept 2:

you have the ability to take the
guesswork out of managing
your people.

Overview

Have you ever hired a smart person with a strong resume and plenty of experience, expecting a certain level of performance, but ending up with something completely different? Do key members of your leadership team have certain traits that may be holding them back from achieving their full potential?

For most mid-market CEOs, the answer is a resounding *Yes*.

This is natural, as humans are imperfect creatures driven by emotion, beliefs, quirks, and irrationalities. And most mid-market CEOs and their HR managers don't realize that approximately 83% of the characteristics of their weakest performers also exist in their strong performers. This highlights the difficulty getting all of your people to consistently perform at a high level—such a small piece of the people-puzzle is the key that determines the difference between a superstar and a dud.

What are other pitfalls of managing people?

- Finding out two years after hiring someone that they're not able to perform as you expect.

- Having the right person in the wrong job. It's not always easy to see that a person underperforming in one position might flourish in another.

- Promoting a great performer through the ranks until they hit their ceiling and fail.

The good news is that over the last 20 years scientific research has begun to unlock many of the complexities of human nature. We've all heard the "nature vs. nurture" argument. Nature is your hard-wiring; it's how you're energized and motivated to perform; it's your built-in guidance system—the thing that moves you. A person who is wired to be highly organized will be that way throughout their entire life, from age 3 to age 43, to age 73. Nature's traits are those that come "factory installed."

The other part, that comes to you through nurture, is learned. This is the part that your parents, your grandparents, your coaches, teachers, and friends, as well as all those who had authority over you as a child, stitched into your mind. These qualities are known as attributes, decisions and injunctions.

- Attributes are those things that people told us we did well when we were young—things we were encouraged to keep doing.

- Decisions help shape us because they are based on what we learned and how we chose to survive in society. They're the choices we made based on our self-perceptions—whether we decided that we're friendly, funny, likeable, etc.

- Injunctions are the rules and practices we were instructed to follow in life—they became our life script.

Psychologists generally agree that approximately 45% of a person's make-up is formed by nature, 45% is formed by nurture, and 10% is a blend of the two. Understanding people from both a nature and a nurture standpoint provides significant insight into whether or not they can change or improve specific facets of their personality.

Mid-market CEOs now have access to effective, scientifically proven employee assessment tools that help to evaluate these types of issues and provide a more complete understanding of a person's potential. These assessments are one piece of the puzzle. If you were to design the perfect employee, assessments could provide about 40% of the data you'd need—but the data that they do provide is the kind that delivers key information employers need to separate superstars from employees who should be avoided.

These assessments are backed by decades of scientific research and have the capacity to:

- Identify and describe the facets of an employee's personality

- Identify leadership qualities and leadership style

- Determine an individual's natural reaction mode to environmental stimuli—their personal behavioral style

- Measure emotional intelligence—the ability to adjust to one's environment

Once thought of as a "soft skill," the ability to assess these characteristics is becoming more quantifiable in many professions—especially in leadership roles—and they play a greater role in overall job success.

The concept of using validated assessments to "map" your people gives you a powerful understanding of who should be doing what within your company, along with the knowledge of what motivates them, where their strengths lie, and how they are likely to react to change and stimuli.

Having this type of protocol in place can dramatically increase your ability to execute company strategy. How many slots do you have for weak performers?

A second vital use of assessments is as a tool to help create a hiring strategy. Your ability to hire great people is potentially your greatest advantage over your competition.

Hire slow and fire fast is an old adage that has proven to be valuable advice for untrained hiring managers. Yet psychologists often suggest that it's human nature to make a decision whether to hire someone within the first ten minutes of the interview. The rest of the time is spent validating the interviewer's decision.

Using a defined hiring process for preparing, sourcing, interviewing, selecting, and on-boarding talent helps eliminate many of the common hiring pitfalls encountered by mid-market companies:

- Putting mediocre employees in charge of hiring

- Allowing personal biases to impact decisions

- Jumping to conclusions

- Misinterpreting resume facts

- Talking too much and not getting answers to key questions

- Failing to check history and references

- Ignoring evident patterns of behavior

- Inadvertently telegraphing answers to your questions

- Getting schmoozed by an intoxicating candidate's personality, résumé, and references

A quality hiring process allows you to combine the opinions of your team members during the interview process. The most complete hiring processes involve 12 essential steps for successful preparation, sourcing, interviewing, selecting, and on-boarding personnel. Proper hiring is critical for companies that want to build a strong culture, and it's an essential practice for any mid-market CEO focused on building a strong company.

Eliminating hiring mistakes enables you to:

1. **Save time** by avoiding sourcing applicants in the wrong places, and interviewing countless numbers of applicants who are neither qualified nor deserving of your time and consideration.

2. **Remove pressure** associated with the sudden rebooting of a hiring system that is designed to work continuously.

3. **Improve margins** by surpassing the average corporate hiring success rate of 58%, and potentially achieving a rate of 85-95% hiring success. Recent studies show that a hiring mistake occurs 82% of the time when a mid-market company hires a new employee, and each mistake costs in excess of four times the annual compensation of the terminated employee.

It's important to clarify that we're not suggesting that you become your own HR department. Most mid-market CEOs give away human resources and the hiring function as early as they can.

We're suggesting that using scientific tools can help you gain a deep understanding of your key leadership team. You're responsible for your people and your culture, and it's your key people who are going to execute, or fail to execute, your strategy. Learn as much about them as possible.

If you implement all four concepts presented in this book you'll find that you are running your mid-market company in a manner similar to the way that Fortune 500 CEOs run theirs. But if you decide to implement only one concept, we strongly recommend that you make it the concept described in this chapter. In the real world, Fortune 500 CEOs don't complete all the activities presented in this book themselves. Their executive teams do it for them. But in lieu of hiring a sophisticated HR executive away from a Fortune 500 company to implement these protocols at your business, we suggest that you own the concept yourself.

You know you've made a "hiring mistake" when one of the following events occurs within 2 years from date of hire:

- The person fires you by leaving the position.

- You fire the person.

- You're unhappy with the person's performance, but they're still working for you.

Activity #1: Map Your People Using a Carefully Chosen Set of Validated Assessments

Personality assessments began gaining popularity in corporate America in the 1960s. And in the past 10 to 20 years, psychologists have made significant scientific advancements in their understanding of what motivates people, how they're hard-wired, and how they react to specific stimuli.

As these assessments have grown in popularity (especially in the context of the Fortune 500), some have come to believe that an assessment can uncover the things that a person does or does not do well. This is not true. No personality assessment can gauge whether or not a person is talented or skilled in a particular area; it can simply reveal tendencies, such as a person's natural inclination toward action or inaction, or how they approach getting what they want. An assessment can identify areas where a person might exhibit high levels of energy versus areas where their energy might be diminished.

This is an important concept. Assessments are valuable tools, but the information they provide is only half the picture. The other half is delivered by understanding how to use this information to motivate and reward people—to find out what really matters to them and how they respond and react to the different types of situations that occur in the workplace every day.

We call this *mapping*—it's similar to a topographic map of a piece of land. A topographic map shows high and low elevations—where it's safe to build and where it's not—and it provides a view of the entire landscape. A complete map of a person is fundamentally different from a report based on a single assessment.

And what do we mean by validation? A validated assessment is one for which there are documented studies and evidence of the assessment's true worth in evaluating personnel. The higher the validation, the more accurate the findings of the assessment will be.

The use of personal computers in the 1980s dramatically increased assessment validation by drastically reducing the time required to factor data and minimizing errors. This led to the creation of new, higher quality assessments that produced more consistent results than older, weaker (and sometimes more popular) assessments.

Validation comes in three forms:

Construct validity — The assessment actually measures what it's designed to measure, and draws meaningful and accurate conclusions on the data. It's measured as a percent of error.

Predictive validity — The assessment predicts future behavior based on data generated at the time of the assessment, and assuming no action taken to change behavioral tendencies, i.e., training or other types of intervention.

Face validity — The premise is that a test-taker will agree with the assessment results if they are satisfactorily explained by a professional, because the results will coincide with the test-taker's personal experiences. Reports generated by these assessments can be easily interpreted, and management team members can be trained and certified in administering the tests and interpreting responses.

The important thing to remember is the difference between validated and unvalidated assessments. Relying on one or two unvalidated assessments can often cause more harm than good.

These scientific breakthroughs deliver something that was almost unthinkable 25 years ago: a blueprint of a person's cognitive and emotional makeup. In the past we've used our instincts and intuition, but today we're able to stop relying solely on intuition and chance, and, instead, use highly-predictive "people mapping" tools to motivate personnel to consistently produce at the highest level.

Here are the five areas where validated assessments are most effective:

1. Assessing the leadership qualities and styles of your key executive team.

2. Assessing your key employees' emotional skills.

3. Assessing what drives behavior and motivates people to take action.

4. Assessing the natural reaction modes or behavioral styles of key personnel in different situations.

5. Assessing the five major factors of your key employees' personalities.

Map the Leadership Qualities and Styles of Your Key Executive Team

Assessing leadership styles can help you to understand your own management style and the management styles of your leadership team members. Leadership styles aren't teachable; they're hard-wired. A good executive team should be comprised of people with a spectrum of management style, representing each of the major styles identified as being most effective.

If you determine that your team does not have a balanced mix of the various leadership traits, you'll have a clear understanding of how to improve it. Having too many people with similar styles can cause problems that hinder execution.

There are many different types of leadership style assessments—some better than others—and it is important to select one for your team that is both validated and reputable.

Leadership styles presented in the Key Management Dynamics Assessment (KMD), created by Objective Management Group, Inc., include the following:

- Visionary

- Strategist

- Innovator

- Developer

- Motivator

- Executor

- Risk Taker

- Negotiator

- Problem Solver

After determining the hard-wired leadership styles that make up your team, the next step is to assess your key people's leadership qualities. Leadership qualities, unlike leadership styles, can be taught, and they can enable key executives to identify deficits in their own leadership skills.

Some important leadership qualities identified by KMD include:

- Business integrity

- Passion for the business

- Open to new ideas

- Is accountable

- Holds others accountable

- Board room presence

- Practical

- Strong work ethic

- Makes difficult business decisions

- Persuasion

- Strong business relationships

- Able to survive business crises

- Reliable and steady

- Team player

- Creative

- Confident

- In search of excellence

No single executive has an abundance of all of these qualities. Many talented, high-performing executives might score high in five to seven of them. The key is understanding which qualities are most prevalent on your team. This will enable you to direct your people in areas where they have the greatest capacity, and eliminate the frustration of expecting something they cannot deliver. It allows you to set them up to be successful.

Map Your Executive Teams' Emotional Skills

Assessing your people's emotional intelligence enables you to understand their social and emotional strengths and weaknesses.

Research has shown that "emotional quotient," or EQ, has become a far greater predictor of workplace success than IQ. Emotional quotient is the ability to sense, understand, and effectively apply the power and acumen of emotions to facilitate high levels of collaboration and productivity. It's our ability to manage our emotions and the emotions of those around us.

In the business environment, EQ is important because it helps leverage awareness of emotions for effectiveness in the workplace. It's been estimated that as much as 90% of work success, once formal education has been completed, is attributable to EQ.

EQ assessments from different vendors are fairly standard, though there are different ways to present them. The Multi-Health Systems EQ-i® assessment evaluates five basic principles of emotional intelligence, broken down into five general areas with 15 skills. These include:

1. IntraPersonal

    a. Self regard

    b. Emotional self-awareness

    c. Assertiveness

    d. Independence

    e. Self actualization

2. InterPersonal
   a. Empathy
   b. Social responsibility
   c. Interpersonal relationships

3. Adaptibility
   a. Reality testing
   b. Flexibility
   c. Problem solving

4. Stress
   a. Stress tolerance
   b. Impulse control

5. General Mood
   a. Optimism
   b. Happiness

While IQ is still important, measuring EQ provides a clear understanding of which people should be interfacing with your market and leading your team, and which people should stay behind the scenes in R&D, production, and technical activities.

Map Your Executive Teams' Emotional Skills

Do you know what motivates your key people to take action? Do you understand the source of their desire to undertake certain activities—or to avoid them? Are you able to understand why your people behave the way they do, and manage in a way that discourages negative conduct?

Psychologists are now able to better understand personal interests, attitudes, and values—the powerful motivating forces that drive behaviors. It's a way to understand "what people really want."

This is the "why" in terms of explaining the things we do. Understanding what motivates your key leadership team members and what drives their behavior provides the key element in understanding how to maximize each person's potential—the framework for presenting and processing information.

Here are six attitudes that are measured in the Motivation Insights Assessment delivered by Target Training International:

Theoretical:
A passion to discover, systematize, and analyze; a search for knowledge.

Utilitarian:
A passion to gain return on investment of time, resources, and money.

Aesthetic:
A passion to add balance and harmony in one's own life and to protect our natural resources.

Social:
A passion to eliminate hate and conflict in the world and to assist others.

Individualistic:
A passion to achieve position and to use that position to influence others.

Traditional:

A passion to pursue the higher meaning in life through a defined system for living.

Once you know and understand which of these attitudes drives the actions of your executives, you'll be able to immediately understand what makes them effective, what gives them satisfaction, and what makes them feel personally successful. You'll also gain insight into what causes conflict amongst them.

Map Your Key People's Natural Reaction Mode or Behavioral Style in Different Situations

After you assess the behavioral styles of your key people, you'll be able to understand how they can adjust their behavior to better suit business situations, so they can avoid communication challenges and reduce stress.

Better yet, you'll gain an understanding of how your key team members will react to situations BEFORE they arise.

Behavior style assessments have a long track record. The most well-known assessment is the DISC quadrant behavioral model based on the work of William Moulton Marston, PhD, in the early 1900s. DISC assessments examine and measure four dimensions of personality that are each associated with a behavioral style:

Dominance:

Assertive and fast-paced

Influence:
Outgoing and personable

Steadiness:
Relaters focused on trust and process

Compliance:
Analytical with desire to get it right

It's rare for a person to have only a single behavioral style—studies have shown that only 4% of the western world has just one. Most people have two, and some have as many as three.

Understanding your team's DISC can help you to understand and appreciate their behavior styles. It can also help them adapt to your style in communicating with others. This enhances interaction between team members, and sheds light on how your executives go about getting what they want.

Map the Five Factors of Your Key Employees' Personalities

Assessing the personalities of your key people allows you to compare and contrast their personality style to the profiles of strong leaders. This gives you the ability to understand which executives possess personality styles that are the best fit for your industry, your company, or your department, and it enables you to create strategies to develop key areas that will make your team stronger leaders.

There is a new movement among psychologists to improve upon some of the perceived shortfalls of popular personality assessments.

For three decades, the training community has generally followed assumptions that rely on factors such as:

- A four-dimension model

- Bimodal distribution of scores on each dimension

- 16 independent types

- The concept of a primary function determined by Judger/Perceiver preference

- A grounding in the personality theory of Carl Jung

The emerging new paradigm is a radical departure from this four-dimensional model, and it requires a significant shift in thinking. It involves the following elements:

- Five dimensions of personality

- Normal distribution of scores on these dimensions

- Emphasis on individual personality traits

- Type concept replaced by blends concept

- Preferences indicated by strength of score

- Model based on experience, not theory

This is called the Five-Factor Model of Personality, and it is the most current, valid, and reliable means available for assessing personality. Psychologists use it as the primary means of understanding and interpreting personality.

The Five-Factor Model is:

Reliable:
Extremely reliable compared to available personality inventories

Acceptable:
High acceptance of personal results by those tested

Respected:
Currently the most widely respected personality model in the personality research community

Valid:
Established predictive validity across a variety of jobs

Uncomplicated:
No theory to understand—a clear vocabulary of individual similarities and differences

Compatible:
Serves as a road map to major theories of personality

The essence of the Five-Factor Model of Personality is that:

- Personality has five dimensions.

- Scores on dimensions will fall along a normal distribution (bell curve).

- Personality is best described by individual traits rather than by type groupings.

- Strength of individual scores indicates personality preferences.

- People scoring in the midrange for a particular trait prefer a balance of the two extremes.

These new five-factor models are strong, validated assessments that deliver an essential component to mapping your people.

Key Takeaway

Use a sequence of validated assessments to gain scientific insights into all aspects of your leadership team.

Activity #2: Coach Your People Based on Assessment Findings

Most mid-market CEOs are fascinated with the assessment reports of their key leadership teams. The reports typically explain many of the nuances they've experienced with their people ... but never quite figured out how to correct or avoid.

To get your people to perform at the highest level, you must apply what you've learned from the assessments in everyday interactions and situations. Your people all have a history, and these histories affect how your culture is shaped.

As you delve into the "maps" of your key leaders, you'll gain a stronger understanding of how to integrate them into a single unified culture. Getting your team to perform at the highest level is a gradual process, and as the coach, it's up to you to move them from base to base.

Would you know if one of your key executives was close to running out of gas, either from hitting the peak of their ability or simply being exhausted? Information from assessments can confirm or refute your intuition and reveal how to coach a player out of hazardous situations. Your responsibility is to move them from Point A to Point B.

If two people are stuck at Point A, getting them to Point B might require different approaches, depending on personality traits revealed in their assessment results. Some CEOs keep diagrams detailing how to work with key executives in specific situations—how to effectively communicate to motivate them to perform at their best in any given situation.

Look at the diagram on the next page. Using the assessments and your own experience, you should be able to determine which of four distinct positional quadrants a person is occupying at any given point in time. Sometimes a person will get stuck in one or another, but most of the time you should be able to coach them to a better position.

People

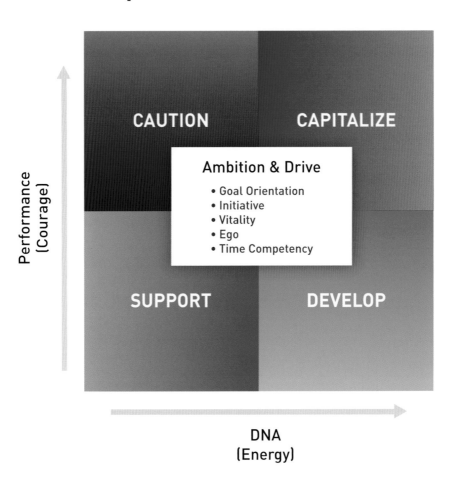

Performance
(Courage)

CAUTION

CAPITALIZE

Ambition & Drive

- Goal Orientation
- Initiative
- Vitality
- Ego
- Time Competency

SUPPORT

DEVELOP

DNA
(Energy)

Here's how to respond to someone, based on their current quadrant:

1. If someone is not pulling his weight, they need support.

2. If someone is doing well but stressed, you must provide caution.

3. If someone is hitting their goals and doing a good job, but not fulfilling his potential, you must provide development.

4. If someone is exceeding all their goals, but not feeling challenged, you must question whether they want to be on your team, and capitalize.

Jim Collins' work in *Good to Great* coined the popular term "get the right people on the bus." Getting them on the bus is half the battle. They still have to be managed.

If you sense that one of your executives is running out of gas, check her assessment. This will provide insight into her high energy and low energy areas. High energy in a particular discipline doesn't necessarily mean that you are good at it; if you haven't been trained, your work might not yet be adequate, but assessment results may indicate that this is an area where you have a lot of energy to learn and grow.

On the other hand, you might be very good at something for which you have very low energy. This would imply that you are using a lot of energy every day, and you are inclined to burn out. Even though you might be doing a good job, it may not be an area where you have a lot of energy to expend over a long period of time.

This is very common. According to Marcus Buckingham, a well-known business speaker, trainer, and author, his studies show that, on average, people spend only 17% of their day in high energy areas and the other 83% of their day in low energy areas. Once you understand what these areas are for each of your team members, you'll have a clearer picture of why they might get tired, angry, and frustrated over time in their job.

This is critical—most people don't work because they want to get rich; they do it because they find their jobs stimulating, engaging, and rewarding. They do it because they enjoy feeling appreciated and on track with their lives. These factors are far more motivating for many people than is money or power. There are exceptions, but the overwhelming majority of people would rather do something that engages and energizes them, even if the alternative might have a bigger paycheck.

Consider the work people perform as they get older. Most move toward work that provides them greater gratification on a personal level, as opposed to work that, though it might be financially more rewarding, does not appeal to their inner aspirations.

Key Takeaway

Eliminate relying on gut-feelings or instinct in managing your key leadership team. Instead, use blueprints delivered by assessments to understand how to best motivate each member of your team, how to structure their roles for optimal performance, how they'll react to specific situations before they occur, and how to prevent conflict that hinders production.

Activity #3: Use a Hiring System to Get the Right People Aboard and Protect Your People Assets

After you've mapped your key leadership team using a carefully-chosen set of validated assessments, the next step is to create a strong filter so that your new hires will fit within your culture and management team and perform at a high level.

In hiring people, the two most important guidelines for building a great company are to:

1. Create high barriers to entry, which is your hiring system

2. Enforce strong accountability

Effective hiring isn't an art; it's a science. When you use a defined hiring process you can eliminate the hiring mistakes that inflate expenses, lower the top line, and hinder a company's execution.

Every organization (whether it's a business, a club, or a church) that creates high barriers to entry and demands strong accountability, along with constant learning requirements, has a chance to achieve greatness. Low barriers to entry, no accountability, and no requirement for advanced learning creates an environment of mediocrity. A strong hiring system is one of the gateways to creating a great company.

We recommend using a hiring system that provides a process for handling four distinct steps:

1. Sourcing the right candidates

2. Properly screening to determine which candidates to interview

3. Structuring interviews to produce specific information needed for hiring decisions

4. Designing an on-boarding plan to get new hires producing immediately

Sourcing the Right Candidates

When searching for candidates, the "shotgun" approach of generating the most respondents is rarely the most effective. When the hiring manager or HR is flooded with resumes, it can cause an egregious waste of time and money. More is not always better. With a precisely targeted approach, you can get highly qualified candidates in the door to speed the screening process.

Properly Screening to Determine Which Candidates to Interview

Some candidates look great on paper, but are not a good fit for the position and aren't worth even an interview. Instead of simply interviewing the candidates who look best on paper, or interviewing everyone and relying on your hiring instincts, it's important to properly screen candidates using predefined criteria and assessments so you need interview only the top candidates for the job.

Structuring Your Interviews to Produce Specific Information Needed for Hiring Decisions

Psychologists suggest that it is human nature to make an unconscious decision as to whether you want to hire a candidate within the first ten minutes of an interview. The rest of the interview is spent looking for reasons to validate that decision. To combat this inclination, use a structured interview process whereby ten different interviewers within your company are able to arrive at the same conclusion. This decreases the potential for human bias and minimizes hiring mistakes.

Designing an On-Boarding Plan to Get New Hires Producing Immediately

You've hired your superstar, so what's the best way to get them producing? Create a structured on-boarding plan that will enable the new employee to learn the job quickly and start producing return for the company. On-boarding plans aren't solely to benefit employers, though. Top talent is always in demand, and you'll send the wrong message to your talented new hires if you leave them to learn the job on their own terms, causing a greater risk of losing them within the first 12 months.

Key Takeaway

Use a structured hiring system to
cover the four key steps for finding
the right people for your company.
This eliminates guesswork and
dramatically reduces your risk
of adding the wrong people and
damaging your culture and
execution ability.

Concept Summary

You have the ability to take the guesswork out of managing your people.

What to *unlearn*

Knowing your key people's struggles, but not being able to alleviate them; not knowing what motivates your key leadership team; hiring people based on gut instinct; not identifying and nurturing your top human assets; hiring based solely on experience or hard skills.

What to *learn*

Use a hiring system involving structured screening, interviewing, and testing; use validated assessments to understand what motivates your key leadership and to understand how they will shape your company culture; measure the EQ of your team; rank your team to understand who are your most valuable assets, who can become valuable assets, and who needs to be replaced.

How the Fortune 500 approach it

Use professional hiring firms, processes, screening, and assessments to "get the right people on the bus" and keep them performing at peak levels.

concept 3:

you must win mind share to influence your market.

Overview

Years ago Peter Drucker, the father of business consulting, made a very profound observation:

> ❚❚ *Because the purpose of business is to create a customer, the business enterprise has two—and only two—basic functions: marketing and innovation. Marketing and innovation produce results; all the rest are costs. Marketing is the distinguishing, unique function of the business.*

Yet the marketing function is broad, challenging, and often misunderstood, especially at mid-market companies. Ask several people to define it and you'll probably get very different answers:

- It's advertising and promotions

- It's brochures and slogans and print ads in magazines

- It's websites and email campaigns

- It's communicating with customers

- It's an MBA crunching numbers on brand equity and market share

Marketing includes the above activities, but it's much more than brochures and websites and numbers. The entire marketing function is an investment that generates revenue, profit, and opportunity for growth. A good definition for marketing is the process of developing and communicating value to your prospects and customers.

Think about every element involved in selling to, servicing, and managing your customers:

- Your knowledge of the market and your strategy to penetrate it

- Your ability to win mind share in the market

- The distribution channels you use to connect with your customers

- Your pricing strategy

- The messages you deliver to your market

- The look and feel of your marketing materials

- The experience you deliver to your market and customers

- Your distinct differentiation and competitive advantages

- The actions of your sales and service reps

- All the preparation, forecasting, and measurement of your marketing investments

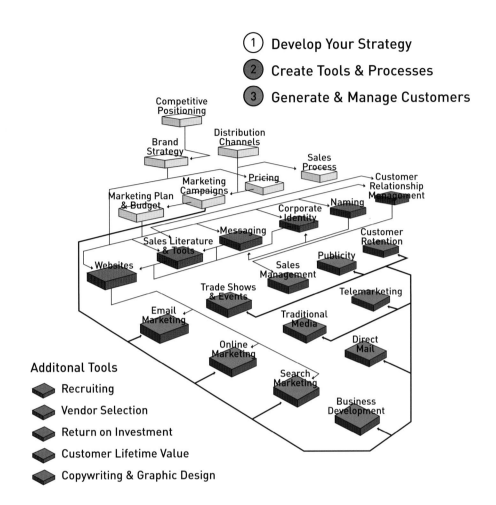

The Fortune 500 and savvy mid-market consumer products (B2C) companies understand this and approach the marketing function from an angle that is fundamentally different from that of most mid-market companies:

> **They start with market research and devise a focused, comprehensive strategy to penetrate their market and build their brand to win mind share before they enter a market.**

The typical mid-market company is focused on sales, a tactical function of the marketing process, and gives little thought to researching the market, building a brand, or winning mind share. When you consider the mindset of the typical mid-market CEO, this makes sense—most were very-skilled and well-trained engineers, salespeople, or finance people prior to either starting their own company or taking over the top role. Few arrive with strategic marketing experience.

> **The typical mid-market company is focused on sales, a tactical function of the marketing process, and gives little thought to researching the market, building a brand, or winning mind share.**

The majority of mid-market companies in the U.S. were started by an entrepreneur who mastered his craft, built a customer base, and achieved growth through business relationships, good sales execution, and local market need.

In these companies the sales team drives the strategy and views the marketing function as a tactical role to provide leads so Sales can hit their revenue targets. Marketing is commonly treated as an expense center, and many marketing functions are often relegated to a creative or administrative person.

The smaller the company, the greater the likelihood that the sales team will rule the roost, and the marketing function will be mistreated. This problem isn't readily apparent in the early stages of companies, as most startup companies begin penetrating their market solely through the sales function. But once growth levels off, it limits sales and forces companies to rethink their strategy.

This isn't surprising, though, and mid-market CEOs shouldn't beat themselves up over it. The reality is that Fortune 500 companies struggle with the marketing function as well. Average tenures of Chief Marketing Officers have been historically shorter than their other c-suite colleagues. The two most-likely explanations are:

1. CMOs don't always speak the same business language as the CEO, the CFO, the COO, and the CTO, and this hurts their presence in the c-suite.

2. When things go wrong, the marketing function is often the easiest to blame. Investors aren't nearly as rattled when a CMO is fired, as when a CFO, a COO, or a CEO of a public company is cut loose.

But the differences between the marketing departments of the Fortune 500 and mid-market companies are clear. The big companies have a Chief Marketing Officer, an array of senior marketing executives, and a large pool of employees and consultants devoted to market research, brand strategy, positioning, distribution, and marketing execution, as well as a healthy marketing budget for media buys.

A typical mid-market company, say a $40 million electrical distributor, may have a marketing director responsible for writing and managing the annual marketing plan, along with a handful of marketing coordinators and creative people, and a small budget for media and outside vendors.

What the mid-market company misses out on when they mistreat the marketing function is leverage—the ability to influence the market on a one-to-many basis. Instead, most focus on incremental growth using the one-to-one sales approach.

> ❞ What the mid-market company misses out on when they mistreat the marketing function is leverage— the ability to influence the market on a one-to-many basis.

If you're not sure which scenario applies to your company, ask yourself two questions:

- Does your marketing and sales strategy work as well as you believe it could?

- Are you influencing your market, or is your market influencing you?

To create a focused strategy to gain leverage and attempt to influence your market, conduct two new activities and change the way you approach a third.

Activity #1: Determine Your Mind Share to Win

What sets your offering and company apart from your competitors? What value do you provide and how is it different than the alternatives? How are you positioned in the mind of the market?

Competitive positioning is about defining how you'll "differentiate" your offering in the mind of your market, and how you'll create value. It's about carving out a spot in the competitive landscape and focusing on delivering on that strategy to win mind share.

When your market clearly sees how your offering is different from that of your competition, it's easier to win mind share and influence your market. Without differentiation, it takes more time and money to show prospects why they should choose you; as a result, you often end up competing on price—a tough position to sustain over the long term.

Your competitive positioning strategy is the foundation of your entire business—it's the first thing you should construct if you're launching a new company or product. It's also important when you're expanding or looking for a competitive advantage.

A good strategy includes:

Market research profile:

Market size, competitors, stage of growth, market segments, and a competitive analysis—strengths, weaknesses, opportunities, and threats in the landscape—along with your market lifecycle

Value proposition:

The method that defines how you deliver value to the market

Dominant competitive advantages:

Clarified, distinguished strengths of your organization

Competitive positioning strategy:

A complete assessment of your current positioning, a determination of the mind share you want to own, and your plan to achieve it

When you put it all together, where do you currently stand in your market? Where do you desire to be in X years in the future? How are you planning to get there? The answers to these critical questions lay the foundation for all of your future market penetration activities: branding, pricing, distribution, market messaging, selling and servicing customers.

Fortune 500 companies employ an army of well-trained employees and consultants to perform market research when crafting their positioning strategy. There's too much money at stake to enter markets without it. Yet it's uncommon for mid-market companies to perform in-depth research, either before entering a new market, or when refining a strategy in an existing market. While many B2C mid-market companies consider the mind share they want to own, few B2B mid-market companies do.

Research Your Market

The first step to creating your competitive positioning strategy starts with market research. This is painful for many mid-market companies and feels like an academic exercise. It is. There's no way to dress it up and make it sexy. It involves surveys, market analyses, competitor analyses, and market segmentation.

It might sound foolish to perform market research in markets where a mid-market company has been operating for years or decades. The reality is that most mid-market executives know the basics of their markets and are very familiar with their nearest competitors, but they have a limited scope of vision. This hinders them as they focus on executing their strategy, and drives them toward tactics to make incremental improvements instead of larger scale strategies to impact the overall market.

In the words of the authors of the best-selling book *Blue Ocean Strategy*, W. Chan Kim and Renée Mauborgne, "this facilitates competing head-on in a bloody red ocean of rivals fighting over a finite customer base and shrinking profit pool, instead of moving into a blue ocean, or uncontested market space ripe for growth."

For those mid-market companies that do endeavor in a detailed market research project, it's not unusual for the executive team to be surprised at the results. Common responses we've seen include:

- Seeing new opportunities that they weren't aware of

- Realizing that they've been aiming too low

- Finding out that their competitors are stronger than they are

- Realizing there is no differentiation between themselves and their main competitors

The value in the market research isn't in the numbers themselves; it's in the conclusions that result from analyzing them. This is standard procedure in big companies, as research is part of any academic exercise that a graduate-level student encounters. And most of the big company researchers have graduate degrees, so it comes to them naturally. Many mid-market executives don't have this type of background; they tend to have deeper hands-on and entrepreneurial experience.

To complete your market research you can either hire a market research firm or handle it in-house. Most mid-market companies have the bandwidth for the latter, so here's the information you'll need to get started:

- Document the size of your market, your major competitors, and how they're positioned.

- Determine whether your market is in the introductory, growth, mature, or declining stage of its life. This "lifecycle stage" affects your entire marketing strategy.

- Understand the problems that your market faces. Talk with prospects and customers, or conduct research if you have the time, budget, and opportunity. Uncover their true wants and needs—you'll learn a great deal about what you can deliver to solve their problems and to beat your competitors.

- Group your market into "segments," or "personas," customers with similar problems who use your product in similar ways. By creating segments or personas, you can efficiently market to each group.

- List your competitors. Include any that also solve your customers' problems, even if their solutions are much different from yours— they're still your competition.

Define Your Value Proposition

After reviewing your market research, begin to think about how you deliver value to the market. Don't think about your selling messages— focus on your method for delivering value.

This will become one of the key elements of your positioning strategy— your value proposition. There are three essential methods of delivering value to your market:

- Operational efficiency (the lowest price)

- Product leadership (the best product)

- Customer intimacy (the best solution & service)

Determine which one you're best equipped to deliver. This is your "value proposition."

These companies are totally focused on delivering their value propositions. They don't just say it—they do it, and that makes it easier to win in their respective markets.

Operational Excellence	Product Leadership	Customer Intimacy
XTC Technology's customers don't want bells and whistles—just a good product at the lowest possible price.	Alpha Co.'s customers care most about quality—they want the best product.	Starboard's market is flooded with products at all ends of the price spectrum.
XTC focuses on operational excellence so they can continually offer the lowest price in the market. For example, they just patented a new machine that dramatically lowers their costs. They're not trying to come up with new or better products; they just want to produce more volume at a lower cost.	Alpha is completely dedicated to innovation and quality. They're constantly working on product improvements and new ideas that they can bring to market. They know what their competitors are doing and are completely focused on staying one step ahead in order to capture a greater share of their market.	Yet Starboard's customers want more than a product off the shelf; they want customized solutions. So Starboard's mission is to know as much as possible about their customers' businesses so they can deliver the correct solutions over time.
XTC's value proposition is operational excellence—they convey it in their messages and in everything they do.	Alpha's culture is all about product leadership, and their prospects see it even before they become customers.	Starboard knows they can't just say "We offer great service." Starboard's team knows they have to deliver on that value proposition in every interaction they have with prospects and customers.

Rather than leaving your positioning and value proposition to chance, establish a strategy. Think impartially about the wants and needs of your market and what your competition offers. You may find an unmet need in the market, or you may realize that you need to find a way to differentiate from your competitors.

As a result, you may decide to promote a different attribute of your product, or you may find entirely new opportunities to create new products and services. Either way, you'll strengthen your business in both the short and long term.

Determine Your Dominant Competitive Advantages

Next, consider the specific strengths of your product, service, or company and how they differentiate you in your marketplace. These are the characteristics that make you truly unique. When you clarify them and shape them to fit specific criteria, they become what we call *dominant competitive advantages*.

A dominant competitive advantage is a clear, concise, and powerful strength that has certain very specific qualities. A competitive advantage is any one, or more, strength that makes your product, service, or company truly unique—they might be similar to those of your competitors, but if you know how to make them dominant, it's easier to win mind share.

Dominant does not necessarily mean different, or even better. Dominant competitive advantages are your strengths that you've learned how to make more precise, more distinguished, and more memorable with the following criteria:

Quantifiable, not arbitrary:
Leave no room for interpretation or individual judgment.

Tangible and concrete:

Use tangible data and concrete facts that are easy to process.

Objective and credible:

Not debatable. Everyone agrees that it is accurate.

Self-centered:

Make sure you're completely focused on yourself. It's how you differentiate.

True and accurate:

Your claim needs to be bulletproof, without any questions as to its veracity.

Focused and simple:

People can remember one idea, not ten. Stay simple.

Not stated by competitors:

Your competitors may be able to say it, but if they not, you can claim it.

Using stories:

They're easy to remember and people see themselves in them.

Contrast:

Black versus White—Right versus Wrong—Before versus After.

Use your strengths that meet most of the above criteria to differentiate yourself in your marketplace.

Determine Your Competitive Positioning Strategy

When you put it all together, where do you currently stand in your market? Where do you desire to be in X years in the future? How are you planning to get there?

These critical decisions lay the foundation for all of your future market penetration activities: branding, pricing, distribution, market messaging, selling, and servicing customers.

Consider all of your market research, your dominant competitive advantages, and the dominant competitive advantages you'd like to achieve, and boil it down to one thing:

What is the mind share you'd like to own?

Then, craft your long-term strategy to achieve it.

Key Takeaway

Determine the mind share you'd like to own. It's your ultimate destination, something you continuously strive for. Complete your market research to determine what you believe you can own, and then craft a strategy to own it.

Activity #2: Create a Brand Strategy

What is a brand? Is it a logo? A name or a slogan? A graphic design or a color scheme?

Your brand is the entire experience the market has with your company/product/service. It's what you stand for, a promise you make, and the personality you convey. And while it includes your logo, your color palette, and your slogan, those are only creative elements that convey your brand. Instead, your brand lives in every day-to-day interaction you have with your market:

- **The images** you convey

- **The feelings and emotions** you create

- **The messages** you deliver via your website, proposals and sales materials

- **The way your employees interact** with customers

- **A customer's opinion** of you versus your competition

Branding is crucial for products and services sold in huge consumer markets. It's also important in B2B because it helps you stand out from your competition. It brings your competitive position and value proposition to life; it positions you as a certain "something" in the mind of your prospects and customers. Your brand consistently and repeatedly tells your prospects and customers why they should buy from you. It's your vehicle to win mind share in the market.

Think about successful consumer brands like Disney, Tiffany, or Starbucks. You probably know what each brand represents. Now imagine that you're competing against one of these companies. If you want to capture significant market share, start with a strong and unique brand identity, or you may not get far.

Best Case	Neutral Case	Worst Case
Prospects and customers know exactly what you deliver.	The market may not have a consistent view or impression of your product and company, but in general you think it's positive.	You don't have a brand strategy and it shows. It's more difficult to communicate with prospects and convince them to buy. They don't have an impression of your product or why it's better.
It's easy to begin dialogue with new prospects because they quickly understand what you stand for.	You haven't thought a lot about branding because it doesn't necessarily seem relevant, but you admit that you can do a better job of communicating consistently with the market.	What you do, what you say, and how you say it may be inconsistent, which might confuse your prospects.
You close deals more quickly because your prospects' experience with you supports everything you say.	You're not helping yourself but neither are you hurting yourself.	Competitors who communicate more effectively have a better shot at closing your prospective customers.
You can charge a premium because your market knows why you're better and is willing to pay for it.		

If you're B2B, there may or may not be a strong brand in your industry. But when you put two companies up against each other, the one that represents something valuable will have an easier time reaching, engaging, closing, and retaining customers. A strong brand strategy can be a big advantage.

> **The Coca-Cola brand was estimated by Interbrand to be worth $68.7 billion in 2009. That's not the estimated value of the company—it's the estimated value of the name.**

Successful branding also creates brand equity—the amount of money that customers are willing to pay just because it's your brand. In addition to generating revenue, brand equity makes your company itself more valuable over the long term.

Your competitive positioning and your mind share goal will shape your brand strategy. By defining your brand strategy and adhering to it in every interaction with your market, you will strengthen your messages and relationships and improve your opportunity to win mind share.

A simple brand strategy includes:

- **Brand Means**

- **Brand Pillars**

- **Human Personality Traits**

- **Brand Promise**

Brand Means

What does your brand currently mean to your customers? What do you want them to say when asked about it?

To define your brand strategy, start by creating three compelling statements describing what your brand should mean to your customers.

Think of as many statements as you can, and then identify the best three. At least two should be directly related to your first value proposition.

Beware of generic adjectives and ideas! The more specific, unique, and powerful the phrase, the better your prospects and customers will understand it. If you can apply the phrase to any of your competitors, then it's not good enough.

Brand Pillars

Your brand pillars are the strongest emotional benefits your brand delivers. To identify yours, start by listing the features and benefits of your product or service. A feature is an attribute—a color, a configuration; a benefit is what that feature does for the customer.

Next determine which benefits are most important to each of your customer segments.

Finally, identify which benefits are emotional—the most powerful brand strategies tap into emotions, even among business buyers.

Personality Traits

The third step is to think of how you'd describe your brand if it were a person. How would you describe that person's personality? Describe these traits, and then convey them in everything you do and everything you create.

115

Brand Promise

The last step is to put it all together to create your brand promise. Branding and positioning experts like Jack Trout and Al and Laura Ries emphasize that your brand should stand for one thing in the customer's mind. You identified the mind share you'd like to own in the previous activity. Now think about how you can create a promise that will enable you to own that mind share.

> ❞❞ You identified the mind share you'd like to own in the previous activity. Now think about how you can create a promise that will enable you to own that mind share.

The strongest brand promises convey value to their target market or customer personas. Think of your promise as your core selling idea—the shortest and simplest way to convey your value to the market. It takes years to decades of delivering your brand promise to the market, via marketing campaigns through different distribution channels, to achieve a singular word mind share of the market, and most companies will never achieve it.

But striving for it is far better than having no plan at all, so brainstorm, decide, and refine.

Key Takeaway

Create a brand strategy that outlines
the experience you'll deliver at every
market touch point. Your brand is the
vehicle to owning mind share and
influencing your market.

Activity #3: Use a Systematic Approach for All Your Marketing and Sales Activities

You've created your strategy. Now, be sure to execute. When you utilize a systematic approach for all your marketing and selling activities, you give yourself a far greater chance to own the mind share you desire and deliver on your brand promise.

Your team will be responsible for the day-in and day-out execution, but you should ensure that they complete the following three steps to align your strategy to their execution:

- Match your pricing to your value proposition and brand strategy.

- Match end-user needs to a distribution strategy.

- Use a defined marketing framework for reviewing selling messages, approving campaign creative, and managing marketing campaigns.

Match Your Pricing to Your Value Proposition and Brand Strategy

Price is one of the classic "4 Ps" of marketing (product, **price**, place, promotion). It's always a part of the marketing mix in B2C. Yet in many B2B companies, marketers aren't necessarily involved in pricing strategy.

Pricing is a complex subject—there are many factors to consider, both short- and long-term. For example, your prices need to:

- Reflect the value you provide versus that of your competitors

- Be based on what the market will truly pay for your offering

- Enable you to reach your revenue and market share goals

- Maximize your profits

When you offer a truly unique product or service with little direct competition, it can be challenging to establish your price. Put together a strong strategy and competitive analysis so you can determine:

- What your prospects might pay for other solutions to their problems

- Where your price should fall in relation to theirs

Your price sends a strong message to your market—it needs to be consistent with the value you're delivering.

- If your value proposition is operational efficiency, then your price needs to be extremely competitive.

- If your value proposition is product leadership or customer intimacy, a low price sends the wrong message. After all, if a luxury item isn't expensive, is it really a luxury?

When your price, value proposition, and brand strategy are aligned, you're in the best situation to maximize revenue and profits.

Match End-User Needs to a Distribution Strategy

How do you sell to your end-users? Do you use a direct sales team? Resellers? A catalog or a website?

Distribution is another of the classic "4 Ps" of marketing (product, promotion, price, **placement** a.k.a. *distribution*). It's a key element in your entire marketing strategy—it helps expand your reach and grow revenue.

Distribution channels are the pathways that companies use to sell their products to end-users. Both B2B and B2C companies can sell through a single channel or through multiple channels that may include:

- **Direct/sales team:** One or more sales teams that you employ directly. You may use multiple teams that each specialize in different products or customer segments.

- **Direct/Internet:** Selling through your own e-commerce website.

- **Direct/catalog:** Selling through your own catalog.

- **Wholesaler/distributor:** A company that buys products in bulk from many manufacturers and then re-sells smaller volumes to resellers or retailers.

- **Value-added reseller (VAR):** A VAR works with end-users to provide custom solutions that may include multiple products and services from different manufacturers.

- **Consultant:** A consultant develops relationships with companies and provides either specific or very broad services; they may recommend a manufacturer's product or simply purchase it to deliver a solution for the customer.

- **Dealer:** A company or person who buys inventory from either a manufacturer or a distributor, and then re-sells to an end-user.

- **Retail:** Retailers sell directly to end-users via a physical store, a website or a catalog.

- **Sales agent/manufacturer's rep:** You can outsource your sales function to a company that sells different manufacturers' products to a group of similar customers in a specific territory.

Your distribution strategy should deliver the information and service your prospects need. For each customer segment, consider the following:

- How and where they prefer to buy

- Whether they need personalized education and training

- Whether they need additional products or services to be used alongside yours

- Whether your product needs to be customized or installed

- Whether your product needs to be serviced

Then consider how to match end-user needs to a distribution strategy.

- If your end-users need a great deal of information and service, your company can deliver it directly through a sales force. You can also build a channel of qualified resellers and consultants. The size of the market and your price will probably dictate which scenario is best.

- If the buying process is fairly straightforward, you can sell direct via a website/catalog or perhaps through a wholesale/retail structure. You may also use an inbound telemarketing group or a field sales team.

- If you need complete control over your product's delivery and service, adding a channel probably isn't the right solution for you.

Use a Defined Marketing Framework for Reviewing Selling Messages, Approving Campaign Creative, and Managing Marketing Campaigns

Crystallizing your marketing framework adds more science around your selling activities. It starts with your sales process—the series of steps you follow as you guide prospects from initial contact to purchase.

After you've defined your sales process for each product/distribution channel, begin to structure your lead generation activities. In many B2B companies, a sales team is the primary method for reaching out to the market. Salespeople call prospects and customers, but they can do only so much in a day. Marketing campaigns can dramatically increase your reach.

A marketing campaign is a series of touches with your market to communicate a key message. The key word is "series" since it usually takes multiple touches for your audience to recognize your message and respond.

Marketing campaigns can include many different media:

- Email, search, banners, and other online marketing

- Publicity

- Direct mail

- Social media

- Telemarketing

- Trade shows and events

- Print, radio, and other traditional media

It's always best to start with your company's annual goals and develop campaigns to meet those numbers.

For example, when you know how many new customers you need, you can calculate how many leads you'll need, and then design campaigns to generate those leads throughout the year.

For each campaign, have your marketing director follow a distinct set of steps:

- Outline how your customers buy.

- Quantify your campaign goals.

- Target your audience.

- Match your campaign messages and creative to your brand strategy.

- Project campaign ROI.

- Measure results.

- Continually test and improve.

At the conclusion of each campaign, record your actual results, and analyze what caused the differences between your projections and your actual results. Learn from each campaign, so you can build your knowledge base for future campaigns.

Key Takeaway

Use a systematic approach for your marketing and sales activities. Your brand and your mind share owned will be defined by the day-in and day-out execution by your team. Standardize it to bring your strategy to life.

Concept Summary

You must win mind share to influence your market.

What to *unlearn*

Having your sales team define your marketing strategy; not gaining any leverage with your message; having sales own marketing; attempting to differentiate based on features or benefits that aren't important to the market; creating ad hoc marketing campaigns; not knowing what mind share you own, if any; not knowing how you're going to achieve the market share you desire.

What to *learn*

Define the mind share you'd like to own; create a long-term plan to own that mind share; understand how you're delivering value to your marketplace; consciously build your brand; find your competitive advantages; have your messaging reinforce the mind share you want to own; support your brand and tout the things your market cares about; use a structured process for designing, planning, and executing marketing campaigns; have marketing and sales work together.

How the Fortune 500 approach it

Have an army of market researchers, planners, and strategists to create long-term plans on how to influence their market.

concept 4:

your team must be able to clearly
articulate your purpose and your
vision.

Overview

Your company's purpose is the single driver of all company activity. It's the reason you, the CEO, come to work each day; it's the reason the company exists—a reason that your leadership team can clearly articulate and the market understands.

That's how it should be, but it's not true for many mid-market companies.

It's easy to think that the company purpose is to return profits to shareholders; however, profits are simply the end result of well-run companies. An effective purpose reflects people's idealistic motivations for doing the company's work and doesn't just describe the organization's output or target customers; it captures the soul of the organization.

Think about organizations widely considered to be great—the United Way, the American Cancer Society, Boys' and Girls' Clubs, St. Jude Children's Research Hospital, Mother Teresa's Missionaries of Charity. It's easy to see their vision and remember what they stand for, right?

Most businesses have a far less altruistic reason for existence, but that doesn't mean they shouldn't operate without a clear purpose and vision. In Concept 2 we discussed how people are emotional beings, and getting the right people on board is the single most valuable activity any mid-market CEO can undertake. We've shown that most people prefer stimulating and engaging work, versus work they have no emotional connection to. Few are able to last in jobs where they're working solely for money—people work for a purpose.

Many people end up composing an internal purpose because their company doesn't appear to have one. Feeling valued, helping others, the artistic reward of creating something from nothing, the thrill of the deal, doing things you love—these are all common purposes people foster internally that keep them motivated in their jobs. People love fighting for a cause they believe in. Purpose is a powerful force.

Companies that are able to unite their people to their purpose operate differently from those that don't. They hire, market, sell, reward, terminate, and expand differently; they treat their customers differently—their purpose is evident in all these activities.

And purpose extends externally to the marketplace as well. In *Follow this Path: How the World's Greatest Organizations Unleash Human Potential*, by Curt Coffman and Gabriel Gonzalez-Molina, Ph.D., the authors studied millions of people—employees and customers—and concluded that emotional engagement is the "fuel" that drives the most productive employees and the most profitable customers. The first two steps on their "path to greatness" are:

1. Acknowledge the role that emotion plays in driving business outcomes.

2. Acknowledge that all employees possess innate talents that can be emotionally engaged.

The authors argue that, in an age where many products and businesses are commodities, the only way to profitably survive is to unleash the human potential among your employees and customers. The authors ask this simple but profound question: *Why would a customer drive past your competition and pay a higher price to purchase your product?* The answer: You have an emotionally engaged customer.

When it comes to purchasing and repurchasing products and services, studies have shown that people are driven more by their emotions than by reason. The same holds true for employees. The surveys presented in *Follow this Path* show that emotionally engaged employees produce more and stay longer than employees who are not emotionally engaged.

Companies have understood for decades that purpose and vision are powerful internal and external drivers. Company purpose and foundational work became very commonplace in the Fortune 500 starting in the mid 1990s. Much of this is due to the lengthy research and findings published by Jim Collins and Jerry Porras in *Built to Last*. We reference their ideas often in this chapter.

Terminology arising from Porras and Collins' work, such as *purpose*, *core values*, *company vision*, *core ideology*, and *BHAGs*, is now commonplace in Fortune 500 companies. It is not commonplace, however, in mid-market companies, even 15 years after it was presented to the business community.

Why?

There are a number of reasons:

- Many mid-market executive teams lack the bandwidth to add exercises of this nature to their crowded schedules, or they lack the budget to hire a consultant to spearhead the project. Fortune 500 companies might dedicate multiple full-time executives to this type of project, while a company founder or key executive of a mid-market company would most likely handle it in his "spare time." It seems that, to many mid-market CEOs, the matter does not warrant the focus and time required to implement this kind of project. It's almost a paradox—the longer the company goes without articulating its purpose and vision, the further it often veers away from it. What seems like a waste of time to many mid-market CEOs is really the opposite.

- Mid-market companies outnumber the Fortune 500 by over 6,200 to 1. Because of the sheer number of mid-market companies, it's tougher for business ideas to gain traction amongst their leadership, whereas ideas can easily go viral in the Fortune 500.

- Executives of mid-market companies often are not as receptive to what some people refer to as "touchy-feely" or "soft" exercises whose value is difficult to track and measure.

- Most mid-market CEOs have spent substantial mind share on leadership development, a concept that they typically support whole-heartedly. From our experience, though, most mid-market CEOs describe their leadership training as their

The HP Way – from *Building Your Company's Vision*, by James C. Collins and Jerry I. Porras. Harvard Business Review, September-October 1996

In Hewlett-Packard's archives, we found more than half a dozen distinct versions of *The HP Way*, drafted by David Packard between 1956 and 1972. All versions stated the same principles, but the words varied depending on the era and the circumstances.

When asked to name the most important decisions that have contributed to the growth and success of Hewlett-Packard, David Packard answered entirely in terms of decisions to build the strength of the organization and its people.

As Bill Hewlett said about his longtime friend and business partner David Packard upon Packard's death in 1996, "As far as the company is concerned, the greatest thing he left behind was a code of ethics known as *The HP Way.*" HP's core ideology, which has guided the company since its inception more than 50 years ago, reflects a deep respect for the individual, a dedication to affordable quality and reliability, a commitment to community responsibility (Packard himself bequeathed his $4.3 billion of Hewlett-Packard stock to a charitable foundation), and a view that the company exists to make technical contributions for the advancement and welfare of humanity.

years on the job—feeling that they've "been there and done that." Experience doesn't always equate to results though, and we've seen very few who lead by defining, describing, and measuring what they expect their people to achieve. While most feel in their hearts and minds that they've already addressed "leadership issues," they've failed to take that final step of effectively communicating their vision throughout their company and the market.

Mid-market CEOs who are learning about company purpose and foundational work for the first time should study it closely and heed the good advice given by business experts who have delivered decades of research on the topic. More succinctly put, you should follow the example of your Fortune 500 peers.

The research that Collins and Porras presented in *Built to Last* proves that strong foundational work—purpose, vision, values, core ideologies—is a key driver of long-term value, so every CEO's executive team should be able to clearly articulate the company purpose and the vision of the CEO.

As Collins and Porras suggest, "Identifying core values and purpose is therefore not an exercise in wordsmithery. You discover core ideology by looking inside. It has to be authentic. You can't fake it."

Clarifying your purpose and establishing your core values and vision are not "nice-to-have" workshops, to be considered only when your team has some extra time; they're necessary components for effectively influencing your market, establishing a strong company culture, and building long-term company value.

Your company's purpose and core values cement a foundation that establishes the framework for how you will influence your market. It delivers a clear set of principles that will galvanize your employees and emotionally connect your business to your customers. As Collins and Porras suggest, "building a visionary company requires 1% vision and 99% alignment."

To align your vision—both internally and externally—so that it clearly articulates your purpose and your vision, conduct the following three activities:

- Clarify your company purpose.

- Define your core company values.

- Build your supporting foundation infrastructure.

Activity #1: Clarify Your Purpose

If you've made it this far, you've probably been thinking about how you'd describe your company purpose. If you and your leadership team can clearly articulate it now, and if it meets the criteria defined in the sections below, then jump ahead to Activity 2 of this concept.

If you're not yet clear, consider these ideas:

- Your purpose is your higher calling—your reason for being. Identify the impact you want your company to make on the world at large.

- A purpose is never to turn a profit. Profit is a byproduct of well-run companies. An effective purpose reflects people's idealistic motivations for doing the company's work. It doesn't just describe the organization's output or target customers; it captures the soul of the organization.

- For individuals, a purpose is the reason they get up each day and live life. For some it's religion; for others it's family; for others it might be a challenge or a cause. Great companies have a purpose just like people do. Think of Disney, Southwest Airlines, or Google. Can you see their purpose?

It's helpful to see examples of the purpose statements of popular companies we all know (from *Building Your Company's Vision*, James C. Collins and Jerry Porras, Harvard Business Review, September-October 1996):

McKinsey & Company: To help leading corporations and governments be more successful

Merck: To preserve and improve human life

Nike: To experience the emotion of competition, winning, and crushing competitors

Sony: To experience the joy of advancing and applying technology for the benefit of the public

Wal-Mart: To give ordinary folk the chance to buy the same things as rich people

Walt Disney: To make people happy

It's easy to mistake descriptions of your product or service for a company purpose. Make sure your purpose never references a product or your market; neither of these may exist in 50 or 100 years. Collins and Porras suggest that your purpose should last at least 100 years and that it should be something that can never be fulfilled—it's like a guiding star on the horizon that is forever pursued but never captured.

This relatively simple concept often presents a challenge to mid-market CEOs after they start evaluating the initial drafts of their company purpose. It's common for them to recite descriptive statements about their products/services and the markets they serve. These aren't true purposes.

A true purpose should meet the following criteria:

- It is not a goal or a strategy.

- It is not tied to your product/ service or to your market.

- It is not tied to revenue, profit, or wealth.

- It is not bound by the constraints of time.

- It reflects your reason for being.

Herb Kelleher, the co-founder and former CEO of Southwest Airlines, knew that staying true to his company's purpose—to democratize the skies—required Southwest to be the low-fare airline. Market researched showed that Southwest customers desired:

- Chicken-salad sandwiches instead of peanuts

- Larger planes

- Access to larger airports

When Southwest managers presented him with recommendations to give their customers what they desired to make them more loyal, Kelleher responded "Will chicken-salad sandwiches, larger planes, and routes to larger airports help us be the low-fare airline? No. We don't need any *(#$ chicken salad sandwiches."

Southwest has an industry record for consecutive years of profitability and its purpose clearly drives its marketing and strategy decisions—a key contributing factor to its financial success.

Concept #4

Companies that operate with a clear purpose tend to have:

- A strong market presence

- Employees who can recite and explain the purpose

- Turnover that is more defined and controlled

- More targeted hiring

Companies that operate without a purpose tend to have:

- Constant changes in direction

- Erratic financial results

- High turnover

- Loss of key leadership every three to five years

- No acquisition strategy or effort

- No risk taken in new products or service

- Drag on company morale in the form of poor team chemistry, customer complaints, and employee dissatisfaction, as seen in employee surveys

Finally, be sure not to confuse your purpose with your core strengths, or your core competence, or your public agenda. What you do well describes your capabilities; not what you stand for or why you exist.

Your purpose is the ultimate reason the market accepts you; it's the essence of why your market presence survives; it's the GPS of your company. When making strategic decisions, always refer to your purpose ask yourself the following questions:

1. Does the decision support my purpose?

2. Does the decision strengthen my purpose?

Key Takeaway

Clarifying your purpose could be the single activity that creates the greatest long-term value for your company. Do not avoid it. Your Fortune 500 counterparts have done it, and research shows that it enhances company value.

Activity #2: Define Your Core Company Values

After clarifying your purpose, the next step is to define your core company values. Your core values and beliefs are at the very heart of what you do each day and over the years.

Core values define your existence. They can serve as a compass for strategic decisions, and they shouldn't change dramatically over time, if at all. To define your core values, think about all the things you believe in as a company. Look inside your company, and involve your leadership team.

When considering your core values, ensure that they meet the following criteria:

- They are timeless.

- They require no external justification.

- They have intrinsic value.

- They are important.

Remember that your core values (along with your purpose) are meant to inspire—not differentiate. You'll clarify your differentiation in Concept 3—*You must win mind share to influence your market.*

How do your core values impact your people? Jack Welch, the iconic former CEO of GE, said that the most dangerous employee is not the rude, insensitive, actively disengaged employee, but the one with the talent who does not hold to the values of the corporation. While the actively disengaged employee will hurt the company, it is those employees who, no matter how talented, are conflicted about the company values that will eventually cause the greatest harm to the company. These are the people Welch would immediately get rid of.

Core Values Are a Company's Essential Tenets*

Merck
- Corporate social responsibility
- Unequivocal excellence in all aspects of the company
- Science-based innovation
- Honesty and integrity
- Profit, but profit from work that benefits humanity

Nordstrom
- Service to the customer above all else
- Hard work and individual productivity
- Never being satisfied
- Excellence in reputation; being part of something special

Philip Morris
- The right to freedom of choice
- Winning – beating others in a good fight
- Encouraging individual initiative

- Opportunity based on merit; no one is entitled to anything
- Hard work and continuous self-improvement

Sony
- Elevation of the Japanese culture and national status
- Being a pioneer – not following others; doing the impossible
- Encouraging individual ability and creativity

Walt Disney
- No cynicism
- Nurturing and promulgation of "wholesome American values"
- Creativity, dreams, and imagination
- Fanatical attention to consistency and detail
- Preservation and control of the Disney magic

*Building Your Company's Vision, James C. Collins and Jerry Porras, Harvard Business Review, September-October 1996

After generating a long list of potential values, identify three to five that truly define what is important to you over the long term. Realize that your team will present different ideas about your core values, and know that not everyone will agree with them or share them. Over time, those people that don't share your values will leave your company when they realize they're not compatible with its core.

At the very heart this issue will define the type of people that come on your team. People band together over values more than they do for anything else; all business partnerships, relationships, and teams are defined in their culture by this one issue. If you hire people who don't agree with your values, you might just as well hire your competitors to give you advice on how to run your business.

How might you determine if your core values are misaligned or unclear?

A company that is hiring based on a set of well defined, clearly articulated values will:

- Fashion their interview process to include questions and opportunities to clarify the values of the prospects and determine if their values are consistent with those of the company

- Include a "Values" session in the new employee on-boarding process so the new employee is able to more clearly articulate the company values

- Set up performance reviews to include some evaluation of the employees' performance as it relates to the company values

- Create reward and recognition programs for employees who demonstrate company values in their daily work and interactions

Companies that do not have clearly defined and articulated values will:

- Experience increased turnover

- Find that hiring people is always a discussion about money

- Achieve lower employee satisfaction scores in their employee surveys

Carefully evaluate your turnover. If it's high, if people's departures are emotional, or if you cannot attract top people with anything but money, it's possible that your 'values' need to be addressed.

Values define your culture by providing both an axis and an anchor for the people who make your company a success.

Key Takeaway

Your core values define your
company culture. They, along with
your purpose, define your core
ideology, which dramatically impacts
the type of people you attract and
how well they perform.

Activity #3: Build Supporting Foundation Infrastructure

The final step is to surround your core ideology with a framework to cement your company's foundation. As Collins and Porras showed with their research, this foundation will remain fixed while your business strategies and practices constantly adapt to a changing world.

❝ *Truly great companies understand the difference between what should never change and what should be open for change, between what is genuinely sacred and what is not.*

This foundation establishes the framework base for how you will influence your market. It delivers a clear set of principles to communicate to the market through your competitive positioning, your brand strategy, and all your marketing, sales, and public relations activities.

A strong foundation increases your commitment to do everything necessary to ensure that your business will be viable tomorrow, next year, and for years to come.

To strengthen your foundation, lead your executive team through the following three steps:

- Complete a standard company SWOT analysis.

- Identify your public agenda.

- Determine the actions that reinforce your core values.

SWOT Analysis

SWOT stands for strengths, weaknesses, opportunities, and threats and is a standard, stodgy exercise that is part of any marketing plan and most strategic plans. It's the boot camp for you and your team. It's not exciting, but it's essential.

The SWOT analysis matrix helps identify what you do well, what you need to improve, external opportunities you should attempt to capitalize on, and external threats that may stand in your way.

When completing your SWOT, post your purpose so your team can see it (because it's your guiding point). Then, with your purpose as your focus, walk your leadership team through a thorough and disciplined discussion of all the strengths, weaknesses, opportunities, and threats to your business.

With all these factors in front of you, you'll be able to map out a plan of action that maximizes strengths and opportunities, while minimizing weaknesses and threats.

Discover Your Public Agenda

Every company has goals. Goals that are written down or publically stated carry more weight than those that are simply spoken. There is also a difference between having an easily achievable goal and committing to a huge, daunting challenge—such as climbing Mount Everest. These types of goals are big, audacious statements that are clear, compelling and memorable. (Jim Collins refers to them as BHAGs—big, hairy, audacious goals.)

Since Collins and Porras found that Fortune 500 executives often interchange BHAGs and purpose statements, we'll refer to their BHAG as your public agenda to further distinguish the two—companies work toward completing a public agenda and then set a new one; a purpose never changes.

A company's public agenda is not only memorable, but it has a clear endpoint—a tangible finish line that people understand. A strong public agenda galvanizes a leadership team and forces a company to operate with vision.

> *I will build a motor car for the great multitude.... It will be so low in price that no man making a good salary will be unable to own one and enjoy with his family the blessing of hours of pleasure in God's great open spaces.... When I'm through, everybody will be able to afford one, and everyone will have one. The horse will have disappeared from our highways, the automobile will be taken for granted ... [and we will] give a large number of men employment at good wages.*
> *-Henry Ford*

To establish your public agenda, look deep into the future to set a compelling goal, a specific achievement to be reached in 20 or 30 years in the future—something spectacular that's almost unthinkable now, yet aligned with your purpose. It must be in step with your purpose, but never declare your public agenda without knowing your purpose.

Here are some public agendas of well-known companies:

Sony: Become the company most known for changing the worldwide poor-quality image of Japanese products.

Ford: Democratize the automobile. (early 1900's)

IBM: Commit to $5 billion gamble on the 360; meet the emerging needs of our customers.

Wal-Mart: Become a $125 billion company in sales in five years. (1990s)

Nike: Crush Adidas. (1960s)

Toyota North American Parts: Reduce operating costs by $100 million, remove $100 million of inventory from the supply chain and achieve a 50% improvement in customer service.

Unlike your purpose or your core values, which never change, your public agenda will change over time, i.e., once you accomplish it. Be sure not to confuse your core values and purpose with your public agenda. It's easy to do, but remember this: purpose is why the company exists, and your public agenda is a goal to be achieved during the course of business.

This is one area where mid-market CEOs have an advantage over Fortune 500 CEOs. Fortune 500 CEOs will often try to align their values and goals with those that have been previously set by the board, by former leaders, by the charter, or by the original founder. It's difficult to give passion and vision to someone else's dream, and it is rare when the CEO of a Fortune 500 is able to give real vision to that public agenda. Why? Because most people know that the CEO will most likely leave the position before the public agenda is ever achieved, and the new CEO will issue an updated one.

CEOs of mid-market companies are often founders or family members of the founder, and it's their purpose, values, and public agenda—they can speak with great passion, quickly alter the course of the company, and make rapid decisions that are consistently in line with the company values and public agenda.

It's the guiding force for a mid-market company, but usually just a general idea for the Fortune 500.

Determine Actions Reinforcing Your Core Values

Your core values won't come alive unless you determine the actions that will bring them to life—actions that are required by the people within the company. Most breakdowns in personal relationships result from differences in values. If you're in a disagreement and the other person's opinion violates your values, your decision is simple. If not, then there are multiple solutions.

Applying this same concept to your company decisions is powerful. You'll have to do more than just list your core values to make them come alive in the hearts and minds of your people.

A value without an associated action to reinforce it isn't likely to come alive within your organization. We recommend the following:

- Post your values: Make your values visible to your people and your market. Print them on large posters and place them in high-traffic areas of your office. Post them on your website. Circulate them in email. Talk about them in meetings.

- Teach your values at every opportunity: Have your key management team incorporate your values into their everyday discussions with their teams. Reference them during key decisions—in customer service, supplier negotiations, marketing and sales, and HR decisions. Make it clear to everyone that if a business decision violates your values, the response will be simple and clear.

- Reward people for demonstrating your values: Be sure your people know when they're adhering to your values. Create a structured reward system—for instance, awarding "points" for specific actions, keeping score, and delivering a valued reward for employees who achieve a certain threshold. Recognition doesn't always have to be monetary; commending people for doing a good job is very rewarding. Also make sure that your managers give ad hoc recognition. Publically acknowledging people when they don't expect it will cement your values into your corporate culture.

Key Takeaway

Support your core ideology by identifying your public agenda and the actions supporting your values.

Concept Summary

Your team must be able to clearly articulate your purpose and your vision.

What to *unlearn*

Thinking that your purpose is a revenue target or earning percentage; thinking that financial goals are the main motivation for your team; thinking that the future will be like the past; thinking that you don't need to inspire your team to accomplish something important; moving quarter-to-quarter focusing on the short-term instead of making a long-term impact.

What to *learn*

Define your company purpose, commit it to paper, and have your leadership team clearly articulate it; determine your core company values; create a public agenda to give you something to strive for; influence your company culture instead of letting it evolve by chance.

How the Fortune 500 approach it

They commit to these "touchy-feely" exercises because they're proven to work. It's the norm, not the exception.

implementing
the
four
concepts

We've now presented the four concepts and the activities required to implement them into your mid-market company.

By this point, our premise for this book should be clear:

> Mid-market CEOs are the forgotten CEOs in the business landscape, running "mysterious" companies with far fewer resources than the big boys have, yet far more resources than small businesses have, so they've clearly outgrown the ability to operate like a small business. Mid-market CEOs are fundamentally different from the big company CEOs, with different levels of training and different end goals. They're seeking specific solutions, relevant information to use in a format they and their team can consume, that produce tangible and sustained success.

Our experience has shown that the fastest way to accomplish this is to master the four concepts we've presented for improving your performance as a CEO and improving the value of the business.

While we believe that the concepts are simple, the work required to implement them isn't simple; nor is it easy. Three of the four concepts involve changing behaviors and having your executive team complete new tasks that require hard thinking and frustrating hours of mental gymnastics.

Running any type of business is difficult, and there's no silver bullet for success. We chose to simplify the concepts—to drive home the high-level points in a tangible format that CEOs can grab onto, remember, and implement.

So many business books talk about generalities that spark the imagination but have little value in the workplace. Conversely, consultants or big-company business experts present solutions that are far too complex and too expensive for the majority of companies to implement. This was the driving factor behind our decision to organize our findings in this fashion.

The Order for Implementing the Concepts

One thing we've learned over the years is that the mid-market CEOs who benefit the most from embracing these concepts are those who are able to implement them the fastest.

So what's considered fast? That depends on your enthusiasm, your drive, and your ability to carve out time from your executive team's schedule, to implement the new concepts. The implementation activities typically each take days to weeks to complete. Then they must be applied and adhered to during the normal course of business.

The human mind has limitations in terms of the amount of data it can accept and process at a given time, so we've found that it's best for companies to commit to scheduling the activities supporting the concepts over a 12-month period. You didn't learn Physics in a day, so don't attempt to implement all the activities immediately. Treat them as a J Curve.

In our business management system, ShortTrack CEO, we deliver the four concepts over a 365-day period via 12 modules that include 60 tools. That's just right for many companies, and too fast for others.

And what's the best sequence for implementing the concepts? In a vacuum, we'd have every mid-market CEO apply them beginning with the highest-level strategy, and progressing to the operational level. That is the reverse of the order in which we presented the concepts in this book.

In our business management system we tie the four concepts to fundamental business areas, or "quadrants." We use quadrants to illustrate a new way for mid-market CEOs to think about the many facets of their business. Instead of addressing 10 to 15 areas that can appear unlinked or disjointed, we organized every business activity into the quadrants, to simplify thinking and create order out of chaos.

Foundation

Your team must be able to clearly articulate your purpose and your vision.

Market

You must win mind share to influence your market.

People

You have the ability to take the guesswork out of managing your people.

Operations

Your CFO is not giving you all the numbers you need to confirm your everyday decisions.

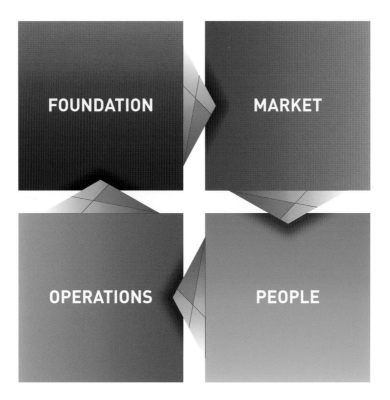

At the highest level, if you implement the concept activities over a 365-day period and measure key information on a dashboard every 30 and 90 days, you should have strong control of the elements driving your company strategy and, ultimately, its value. In our system we use what's called 30 / 90 vision, a focus on key activities every 30 days and a measurement of success indicators every 90 days.

We recommend that you budget a minimum of 10 hours' time per month during implementation. Your executives' time commitment will be greater, and it will depend upon their existing resources and their skills at implementing the activities.

Since we don't live in a vacuum, and mid-market CEOs are challenged for bandwidth, it's fine to jump around and tackle specific activities from different concepts if they can be used to solve an immediate problem. Some of them are intrinsically valuable; some are tied to others and should be completed in sequence.

Here's a list of the activities that can stand alone and can be completed first:

Concept #1 Activity: Foundation | Clarify Your Purpose

Concept #3 Activity: People | Map Your People Using a Carefully Chosen Set of Validated Assessments

Concept #4 Activity: Operations | 24 Month Rolling Forecasting

Concept #4 Activity: Operations | J Curve Management

Concept #4 Activity: Operations | Operational Decision-Making Models

All the other activities in the Foundation, Market, and People quadrants should follow Clarify Your Purpose, as they're inherently linked to it and will build upon it.

Diagnosing Which Concept Will Solve Your Business Problem

How might you diagnose which concept will yield the most impact, or the quadrant that is giving you the most pain? Consider the following symptoms. Are you feeling any of them?

- Instability and severe uncertainty about your business model

- The hunger for more customers—caused by a steep decline in sales

- The stress and frustration of not having your people on the same page as you—they're simply not executing your strategy the way you feel they should and they're fighting you over it.

- Chaos from having too much activity—you're overwhelmed with your current operations and array of projects, and you're worried that you've bitten off more than you can chew.

Result	Symptom	Antidote
Collapse	Instability and severe uncertainty about your business model	Your team must be able to clearly articulate your purpose and your vision—your company **Foundation**.
Starve	The hunger for more customers—caused by a steep decline in sales	You must win mind share to influence your **Market**.
Suffocate	The stress and frustration of not having your people on the same page as you—they're simply not executing your strategy the way you feel they should and they're fighting you over it	You have the ability to take the guesswork out of managing your **People**.
Choke	Chaos from having too much activity—you're overwhelmed with your current operations and array of projects, and you're worried that you've bitten off more than you can chew	Your CFO is not giving you all the numbers you need to confirm your everyday decisions. You must obtain them to improve the performance of your **Operations**.

High Profile Companies Forced into Bankruptcy Due to Meltdown in a Business Quadrant

Result	Example
Collapse	Enron: In 2001, the world's leading electricity, natural gas, communications, pulp and paper company, with claimed revenues of over $100 billion the year prior, claimed bankruptcy in one of the most stunning corporate collapses up to that time. The accounting and fraudulent activity that sank Enron resulted from a shift in the company's foundation starting in the mid 1990s, when company leadership made the decision to shift from being an asset-based utility infrastructure company to a financial trading company. The new philosophy created a trading mentality of profit at any cost. This shift in purpose, and the resulting core values, were the two factors that perpetuated the fraud that destroyed the company.
Starve	General Motors: In 1954, GM held a 54% market share of the U.S. auto market. In 2010 that number had slipped to 19%. While some point to labor issues and a slow economy to explain GM's ultimate bankruptcy in 2009, the long, slow decline in sales due to poor positioning of its brands and weak products caused the company to starve to the point where sales couldn't support its fixed and variable costs.
Suffocate	WorldCom: In 2002, the second largest long distance phone company in the United States declared bankruptcy in the wake of massive accounting scandals that inflated the company's assets by as much as $11 billion. It was the largest such filing in U.S. history at the time. The company, under the direction of its CEO, CFO, controller, and director of general accounting, purposely inflated revenues with bogus accounting entries and underreported costs in a scheme to prop up its stock price. The culture extended all the way to the board of directors, who approved in excess of $400 million in loans to its CEO, Bernard Ebbers, to finance his personal interests.
Choke	Rolls-Royce: As outlined in the Concept 1 chapter, Rolls-Royce, the U.K. based company known for quality since its founding in 1906, declared bankruptcy in 1971 after a five-year run wherein it engaged in far too many J Curves at one time, the most visible being the RB-211 jet engine (which, after the bankruptcy, continued to power jets around the world for decades).

What to *unlearn*

Diving into operations or your area of expertise when times get tough instead of diagnosing the real issue and creating a plan to correct it; not checking your intuition; delegating the 4 key areas CEOs should own; shying away from an area because it's new or unknown; pretending that you have all the answers; being afraid to be wrong or make a mistake.

What to *learn*

Being able to determine which area is causing a business struggle—whether you're collapsing, starving, suffocating or choking, and understanding how to fix it; understanding how the 4 areas tie together and how to use them in your daily work.

achieving ultimate success:

the 5 CEO personas and how they apply the 4 concepts

Many of you aren't feeling any of the symptoms—the warning signs of serious trouble—and are just looking for ways to improve your business and achieve your endgame.

What are the common endgames? In our work with more than 2,000 mid-market CEOs, we've found that their desired endgame dictates their attraction to, and emphasis on, the concepts. We've encountered five common endgames, constituting five specific CEO personas. Each persona applies different levels of focus to the four concepts, based on his or her personal goal, to create their own ShortTrack.

Which one are you?

The Growth CEO	You have a desire to move forward, to get bigger, to expand, to beat your competition and win the game. While this seems to be the logical profile of all CEOs, that isn't what we've experienced—approximately 30% of the CEOs we encounter are true 'growth CEOs.'
The Hired Gun CEO	You've been brought into a new company with the goal of making a short term, immediate impact. It's usually a turnaround or preparation for a company sale, and you have a big financial gain at stake and a reputation for being a turnaround expert. Approximately 15% of the CEOs we encounter fall into this persona.
The Strategic CEO	You're striving for a mid-term exit in 10 years. You're either a company founder, or you've run the company a long time—and you're focused on improving the business, to sell or transfer to a family member. Approximately 20% of the CEOs we encounter fall into this persona.

The Career CEO	You're a new CEO within the first three years of taking on your first command and have achieved your dream role—you plan on being a CEO for multiple companies over your career. Approximately 10% of the CEOs we encounter fall into this persona.
The Auto-Pilot CEO	You've achieved continued success with your business but it requires all of your attention to operate the company at your desired level. You'd like to get the business to the point where it can perform at this level without your constant involvement, so you can work less and have more time for other activities. Approximately 25% of the CEOs we encounter fall into this persona.

Your level of focus on the four concepts ultimately depends on your CEO persona. Here are the concepts and quadrants that each persona focuses on to achieve the endgame:

CEO Persona	Goal	ShortTrack
Growth CEO	Build a bigger company.	75% Market + 15% Operations + 10% Foundation
Hired Gun CEO	Turn around a company in a short period of time.	65% Operations + 20% People + 15% Market
Strategic CEO	Build value for an exit within six to ten years.	25% Foundation + 25% Market + 25% People + 25% Operations
Career CEO	Enhance skills to be able to run other companies.	Focus on your weakest concepts.
Auto-Pilot CEO	Have existing company continue current performance with less time commitment.	Focus on your company's weakest concepts.

As you consider your CEO persona, your personal goals, and the concepts we've presented, remember a final important point that we've learned over the years from our experiences working with CEOs and being CEOs: The key to being a successful mid-market CEO isn't product knowledge or industry experience.

That's what your executive team and managers are for. The key to being a successful mid-market CEO is to understand and carefully manage the most important elements that affect the business value. While the nuances change from company-to-company and industry-to-industry, the high-level concepts are the same. They're the concepts we've outlined in this book.

CEOs with the skills to implement the concepts are qualified to run any mid-market company—and should achieve a high degree of success.

No matter how long you've been running your current company, when you implement these four concepts, things will change. You will:

- Change the way you think about elements of your business

- Change the way you operate

- Feel different

- Make clearer decisions

- Hire better people

- View your market differently

- Notice that your market views you differently

- Get resistance from your team

- Elevate your performance

- Do a better job executing your strategy

- Enhance your skill set

- Enhance your executive teams' skill set

- Increase your company value

- Move closer to your endgame

We wish you success on your journey!

What to *unlearn*
Not having a succinct plan to achieve your endgame.

What to *learn*
Focus on the concepts that are most relevant to your CEO persona.

about
the
authors

Ken Edmundson

For more than 20 years, Ken Edmundson has created, refined, and used techniques and insights that enable mid-market companies to grow consistently and profitably.

Ken is a gifted and insightful master of the business mind and is extremely knowledgeable about directing strategy, people, and execution. A former CEO of a $300 million company, he is currently Chairman of a $100 million company. Ken definitely puts into practice what he preaches.

For six years Ken also held the highly respected position of Chair for Vistage International, the world's largest member organization for CEOs. Ken is a highly trained and sought after mentor and trainer for CEOs of mid-market companies. His innovative and creative uses of technology, his pioneering of behavioral and talent assessments to properly target individuals for their highest energy positions, and his aggressive and forward looking leadership and coaching are indicative of his style.

Ken is also the founder, Chairman, and CEO of the Edmundson Northstar Business Research and Training Institute. The firm is a recognized specialty consultancy in the development of business strategy, leadership, sales and sales management training, and customized employee assessments for companies across a multitude of industries.

From 1989 through 1998, Ken served as Partner, Chairman, and CEO of LEDIC Management Group, Inc. He led LEDIC to become one of the ten largest and most successful multi-family property fee-management companies in the U.S., and then led a very successful sale of the company to a Wall Street investment firm.

Prior to his position at LEDIC, he was President and Chief Operating Officer of Dunavant Development Corporation and a shareholder in the parent company, Dunavant Enterprises, Inc., the 82nd largest privately held company on *Forbes*' list of *Top 100 Private Companies*. Ken also served for six years as President and Chief Operating Officer of Memphis Aero Corporation, a successful chain of general aviation fixed-base operations and the world's largest distributor of Piper aircraft parts. He was instrumental in leading the negotiation and successful sale of the company to AMR Corporation, the parent company of American Airlines.

Ken began his career in 1975 with Martin Industries, Inc., of Alabama, a large privately held manufacturing firm with sales throughout the U.S. and Canada. At the age of 25, he assumed the responsibility of National Sales Manager and Product Director of a division with a 104-person sales force.

Ken's success in building large, service-driven, employee-motivated companies has led to his recognition as a prominent speaker, teacher, and trainer on the subjects of *The Complete and Effective Salesperson*, *The Honorable Way to Sell*, *The Perfect Employee*, *Teamwork*, *Listen! You're Trying to Tell You Something*, *Communication*, and *Business Strategy*.

Jim Sagar

Jim Sagar is the CEO and co-founder of Moderandi Inc, creator of Marketing M.O. (**www.marketingmo.com**) and Growth Panel (**www.growthpanel.com**), websites delivering tools and infrastructure to enable mid-market businesses to structure and execute their go-to-market activities.

Jim has 15 years' experience leading small to medium-sized businesses in marketing, sales, and strategy. An entrepreneur at heart, Jim has been a member of the founding executive team for three startups prior to co-founding Moderandi in 2004.

Jim has worked with more than 200 SMB leaders and marketing consultants, instilling a structured marketing process to turn their ad-hoc marketing activities into a defined strategy that relies upon business logic to answer the hundreds of marketing and sales decisions mid-market company leaders encounter throughout the year.

Jim holds a B.A. of Economics and Communications from the University of Michigan.

Nick Setchell

Nick Setchell is CEO of Practice Strategies, a business improvement consulting firm that defined and developed Fiscal Focus®.

Nick has analyzed in excess of 1,000 businesses and worked with hundreds of CEOs and executives around the world to help them better understand their business performance and make better business decisions.

Practice Strategies has presented in excess of 500 workshops to CEOs and executives in Australia, the US, the UK, Canada, and New Zealand.

Nick has also run numerous coaching workshops for commercial bankers in Australia and the US and senior members of the Australian accounting profession.

Nick has held executive positions in business management for 23 years. For the past 10 years he has been running his own consulting practice, primarily working with CEOs and senior executives.

As a speaker and presenter, Nick has been internationally recognized and has been awarded the "Mick Robertson Award" from TEC Australia, the "Speaker of the Year Award" from TEC Australia, the Vistage UK "International Speaker of the Year Award," and has been recognized by Vistage USA as one of the top 12 speakers of the year out of more than 500 of his peers.

Nick holds a Bachelor of Economics from the University of Adelaide, is a fellow of the Australian Institute of Company Directors, and has been awarded the accreditation "Certified Speaking Professional" from the National Speakers Association of Australia.